W9-AWY-832

Aleene's® Something from Nothing: Treasures from Trash
from the *Best of ALEENE'S CREATIVE LIVING® Series*

Book Division of Southern Progress Corporation
P.O. Box 2463, Birmingham, Alabama 35201

Published by Oxmoor House, Inc., and Leisure Arts, Inc.

Library of Congress Catalog Card Number: 98-65255
Hardcover ISBN: 0-8487-1673-6
Softcover ISBN: 0-8487-1674-4
Manufactured in the United States of America
First Printing 1998

Designs by Heidi Borchers

Editor-in-Chief: Nancy Fitzpatrick Wyatt
Senior Crafts Editor: Susan Ramey Cleveland
Senior Editor, Editorial Services: Olivia Kindig Wells
Art Director: James Boone

Aleene's® Something from Nothing: Treasures from Trash
Editor: Margaret Allen Price
Copy Editor: L. Amanda Owens
Senior Photographers: Sylvia Martin, John O'Hagan
Photographer: Brit Huckabay
Photo Stylist: Linda Baltzell Wright
Illustrator: Kelly Davis
Designer: Alison Turner Bachofer
Senior Production Designer: Larry Hunter
Publishing Systems Administrator: Rick Tucker
Production and Distribution Director: Phillip Lee
Associate Production Manager: Theresa L. Beste
Production Assistant: Faye Porter Bonner

Tree Trimmings on page 62

We're Here for You!
We at Oxmoor House are dedicated to serving you with reliable information that expands your imagination and enriches your life. We welcome your comments and suggestions. Please write us at:

Oxmoor House, Inc.
Editor, *Aleene's Something from Nothing*
2100 Lakeshore Drive
Birmingham, AL 35209

To order additional publications, call
1-205-877-6560.

Cover portrait of Aleene Jackson and Heidi Borchers by Christine Photography

Contents

Painted Pansy Mat on page 28

Star Tree Topper on page 60

Decorative Birdhouse on page 134

Introduction

I believe we need to recycle everything we possibly can to keep things from adding to the already overfull landfills throughout the world. As you'll see by looking at the ideas in this book, there are many wonderful and creative designs we can make with items that would normally end up in the trash. This concept also applies to furniture that may be outdated: by painting or decorating a timeworn piece, you can give it new life and keep it from the trash heap.

We need to teach our young people to be creative. Using salvaged trash items in teaching crafts is an excellent way to challenge the imagination of a child. You'll be amazed at the ideas a few recycled items will bring forth from kids. My grandchildren Austin, 8, and Savannah, 5, often raid my boxes of recyclable items for craft projects and toys, and they spend more time playing with these than with their store-bought playthings. Just the other day Austin pulled a plastic hanger from the recycle bin because he saw its potential as a spaceship. If we can teach children to recycle for craftmaking supplies, we'll not only help the environment but also encourage kids to think creatively.

As I designed the projects for this book, I kept in mind that you won't always be able to find the exact items for your crafts. I've included a wide variety of techniques so that you can use your imagination to adapt these ideas to your furniture or recycled objects. I hope you'll enjoy transforming trash into treasures to decorate your home or to give as gifts.

Heidi

Crafting Hints

Heidi offers her time-tested tips for successful crafting.

Tips for Successful Gluing

To make Aleene's Tacky Glue™ or Aleene's Designer Tacky Glue™ even tackier, leave the lid off for about an hour before using it so that excess moisture evaporates.

Too much glue makes items slip around; it does not provide a better bond. To apply a film of glue to a project, make a cardboard squeegee by cutting a 3" square of cardboard (cereal box cardboard works well). Then use this squeegee to smooth the glue onto the craft material.

Temporary Tape Tip

To apply consistent fine lines of glue to a project, refer to the diagrams below to make a tape tip for your glue bottle.

1. Using 4"-long piece of transparent tape, align 1 long edge of tape with edge of nozzle. Press tape firmly to nozzle to prevent leaks.
2. Rotate bottle to wrap tape around nozzle. Tape will reverse direction and wind back down toward bottle.
3. Press tail of tape to bottle for easy removal.

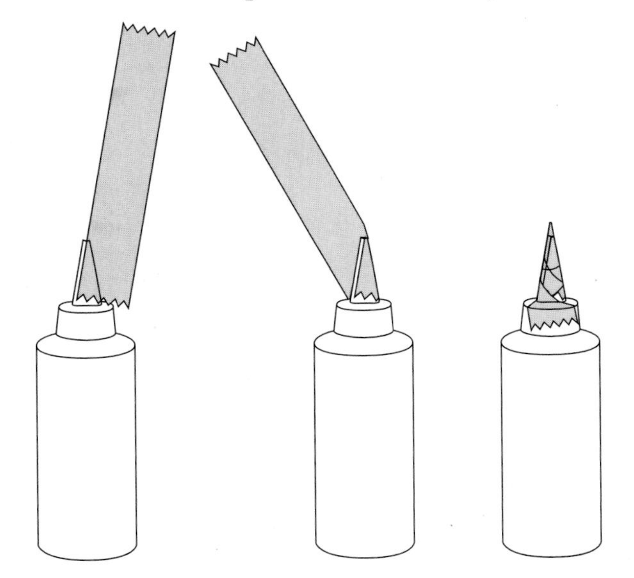

Metric Conversion Chart

U.S.	Metric
1/8"	3 mm
1/4"	6 mm
3/8"	9 mm
1/2"	1.3 cm
5/8"	1.6 cm
3/4"	1.9 cm
7/8"	2.2 cm
1"	2.5 cm
2"	5.1 cm
3"	7.6 cm
4"	10.2 cm
5"	12.7 cm
6"	15.2 cm
7"	17.8 cm
8"	20.3 cm
9"	22.9 cm
10"	25.4 cm
11"	27.9 cm
12"	30.5 cm
36"	91.5 cm
45"	114.3 cm
60"	152.4 cm
1/8 yard	0.11 m
1/4 yard	0.23 m
1/3 yard	0.3 m
3/8 yard	0.34 m
1/2 yard	0.46 m
5/8 yard	0.57 m
2/3 yard	0.61 m
3/4 yard	0.69 m
7/8 yard	0.8 m
1 yard	0.91 m

To Convert to Metric Measurements:

When you know:	*Multiply by:*	*To find:*
inches (")	25	millimeters (mm)
inches (")	2.5	centimeters (cm)
inches (")	0.025	meters (m)
feet (')	30	centimeters (cm)
feet (')	0.3	meters (m)
yards	90	centimeters (cm)
yards	0.9	meters (m)

Working with Aleene's Fusible Web

Always wash and dry fabrics to remove any sizing before applying fusible web. Do not use fabric softener in the washer or the dryer. Lay the fabric wrong side up on the ironing surface. A hard surface, such as a wooden cutting board, will ensure a firm bond. Lay the fusible web, paper side up, on the fabric (the glue side feels rough). With a hot, dry iron, fuse the web to the fabric by placing and lifting the iron. Do not allow the iron to rest on the web for more than 2 or 3 seconds. Do not slide the iron back and forth across the web.

Transfer the pattern to the paper side of the web and cut out the pattern as specified in the project directions. To fuse the cutout to the project, carefully peel the paper backing from the cutout, making sure the web is attached to the fabric. If the web is still attached to the paper, re-fuse it to the fabric cutout before fusing it to the project. Arrange the cutout on the project surface. With a hot, dry iron, fuse the cutout to the project by placing and lifting the iron. Hold the iron on each area of the cutout for approximately 60 seconds.

Sponge-painting How-tos

For allover sponge-painting like the packing-foam frame on page 93 or the colander wind chimes on page 140, dip a small sponge piece into water to dampen it and wring out the excess water. Pour separate puddles of each color of acrylic paint onto waxed paper. Dip the sponge into the first color of paint. Blot the excess paint on a piece of paper towel to keep from applying too much paint at a time. Lightly press the sponge onto the project surface. Repeat until you get the desired effect, painting small areas at a time and applying the paint in a random pattern. Rinse the sponge thoroughly before dipping it into the next paint color. For the best effect, apply each layer of paint sparingly, leaving some areas unpainted and overlapping the paint colors a bit. Be sure to let each color of paint dry before applying the next color.

To paint a project with a sponge shape, such as for the tray on page 40 or the wastebasket on page 142, you'll need a piece of pop-up or compressed craft sponge (available in crafts stores). Cut the specified pattern from the dry, flat sponge. Dip the sponge shape into water to expand it and wring out the excess water. Pour out a puddle of acrylic paint onto waxed paper. Dip the sponge shape into the paint. Blot the excess paint on a piece of paper towel. Lightly press the sponge shape onto the project in the desired position, being sure all areas of the sponge come in contact with the project surface. Carefully lift the sponge off the project. Reapply paint to the sponge shape as needed to continue painting. If the sponge becomes saturated with paint, rinse it thoroughly in water and wring out the excess water before dipping it into paint again.

Cut a shape from a pop-up craft sponge to paint designs on a project.

Foam-Stamping How-tos

You'll find it easy to add a stamped design to a craft project with these directions for making stamps from Fun Foam. See pages 16, 28, and 83 for designs featuring this technique.

To make a stamp, cut the specified shape or shapes from Fun Foam. Center and glue the foam shape onto a piece of foam-core board that is at least ½" larger all around. Let the glue dry. For small foam pieces, such as the star and the heart used for the children's furniture on page 14, glue the foam shape onto a pencil eraser instead of onto foam core.

Brush the foam design with the desired color or colors of acrylic paint. To use more than 1 color on a stamp, simply apply a different color to each desired area of the stamp. Don't apply the paint too thickly because it will smear. Place the stamp on the printing surface and press firmly, being sure all areas of the stamp come in contact with the printing surface. Do not rock the stamp or let it slip around. Carefully lift the stamp off the project. Apply a fresh coat of paint after each printing. To apply different colors to the stamp, wipe the stamp with a damp paper towel, let the stamp dry, and then apply the new colors.

To get the best results, always stamp on a firm, level surface. If your stamp begins to lose detail, wipe the excess paint from the stamp with a paper towel and use a toothpick to scrape any paint from the crevices and the corners of the design.

Brush a thin coat of paint onto the foam design.

Press the stamp onto the printing surface and then carefully lift the stamp off.

Creative Decor

Shop thrift stores and garage sales or rummage through your mother's attic to get inexpensive furniture and accessories for your home. Flip through the following pages for doable ways to turn your bargain buys into a decorator's dream.

A Fresh Coat of Paint

With a little paint, an old wooden chair gets a second life. For the side table, attach a painted plywood round to the top of a wooden stool. Or simply paint a set of stools for seating at your kitchen counter.

Materials

- **For each:** Furniture stripper (optional)
- Fine-grade sandpaper (optional)
- Tack cloth
- Flat white spray paint
- Sponge paintbrush
- Aleene's Premium Designer Brushes™: shader, liner
- Pop-up craft sponges
- Waxed paper
- Clear spray polyurethane finish
- **For chair:** Wooden chair
- **For chair and table:** Aleene's Premium-Coat™ Acrylic Paints: Soft Sage, White, Soft Fuchsia, Soft Lavender, Soft Violet, Soft Blue, Dusty Sage, Dusty Fuchsia, Dusty Lavender, Dusty Violet, Dusty Blue, Deep Sage
- **For table:** Wooden stool
- 23¾"-diameter circle ½"-thick plywood
- Cotton swabs
- 4 (1½"-long) bolts (See note in Step 6 of table directions.)
- **For stool:** Wooden stool
- Aleene's Premium-Coat™ Acrylic Paints: White, Soft Blue, Dusty Sage, Dusty Blue, Deep Sage, Soft Fuchsia
- Cotton swabs

Directions for chair

1. If needed, strip old paint and finish from chair. If needed, sand chair. Wipe chair with tack cloth to remove any dust. Spray-paint chair white to prime. Let dry. Referring to photo for color placement, paint chair with 1 or 2 coats of Soft Sage and White for base coat, letting dry between coats.

2. Transfer patterns on page 13 to pop-up craft sponges and cut 1 large flower, 1 medium flower,1 small flower, 1 round flower, 1 large leaf, 1 medium leaf, and 1 small leaf. Cut 1 (⅝") square from pop-up craft sponge. Dip each sponge shape into water to expand and wring out excess water.

3. Pour separate puddles of paint onto waxed paper. Dip large flower sponge into Soft Fuchsia and blot excess paint on paper towel. Referring to photo for placement, press sponge onto chair to paint large flowers.

Let dry. In same manner, paint medium flowers with Soft Lavender, small flowers with Soft Violet, round flowers with Soft Blue, leaves with Dusty Sage, squares on chair back with Soft Sage, and squares around rim of seat with White. Let dry. Rinse each sponge thoroughly before dipping into different paint color.

4. Paint details on sponge-painted designs with liner brush, using colors as follows: Dusty Fuchsia for large flowers, Dusty Lavender for medium flowers, Dusty Violet for small flowers, Dusty Blue for round flowers, and Deep Sage for leaves. Let dry. Paint vines and tendrils, using liner brush and Deep Sage. Let dry. Spray chair with 1 or 2 coats of finish, letting dry between coats.

Directions for table

1. If needed, strip old paint and finish from stool. If needed, sand stool legs and plywood circle. Wipe stool and plywood with tack cloth to remove any dust. Spray-paint stool legs and plywood white to prime. Let dry. Paint plywood and stool legs with 1 or 2 coats of White acrylic paint for base coat, letting dry between coats. Center and paint 1 (12"-diameter) circle on 1 side of plywood with Soft Sage. Let dry.

2. Transfer patterns to pop-up craft sponges and cut 1 large flower, 1 medium flower, 1 small flower, 1 round flower, 1 large leaf, and 1 small leaf. Cut 1 (5/8") square from pop-up craft sponge. Dip each sponge shape into water to expand and wring out excess water.

3. Pour separate puddles of paint onto waxed paper. Dip large flower sponge into Soft Fuchsia and blot excess paint on paper towel. Referring to photo for placement, press sponge onto plywood to paint large flowers. Let dry. In same manner, paint medium flowers with Soft Lavender, small flowers with Soft Violet, round flowers with Soft Blue, leaves with Dusty Sage, and squares around edge of plywood with Soft Sage. Let dry. In same manner, sponge-paint round flowers and small leaves on stool legs.

4. Paint details on sponge-painted designs with liner brush, using colors as follows: Dusty Fuchsia for large flowers, Dusty Lavender for medium flowers, Dusty Violet for small flowers, Dusty Blue for round flowers, and Deep Sage for leaves. Let dry. Paint vines and tendrils, using liner brush and Deep Sage. Let dry.

5. To paint dots on stool, dip cotton swab into Soft Fuchsia and dot on stool in desired positions. In same manner, add Soft Fuchsia and Soft Blue dots to sponge-painted floral design on plywood. Paint 1 dot of Soft Fuchsia or Soft Blue on each sponge-painted square, centering dot on square and alternating colors. Let dry.

6. Spray painted areas of stool and plywood with 1 or 2 coats of finish, letting dry between coats. (*Note:* Measure thickness of stool seat and plywood circle to be sure that 1½"-long bolt will go through stool seat and into—but not all the way through—plywood.) To attach plywood to stool, lay plywood right side down on padded work surface. Center stool seat on wrong side of plywood. Working from bottom

of stool seat, screw each bolt through stool seat and into plywood, spacing bolts evenly around stool, about ½" from outer edge of seat.

Directions for stool

1. If needed, strip old paint and finish from stool legs. If needed, sand stool legs smooth. Wipe stool legs with tack cloth to remove any dust. Spray-paint stool legs white to prime. Let dry. Paint stool legs with 1 or 2 coats of White acrylic paint for base coat, letting dry between coats.

2. Transfer patterns to pop-up craft sponges and cut 1 round flower and 1 small leaf. Dip each sponge shape into water to expand and wring out excess water.

3. Pour separate puddles of paint onto waxed paper. Dip round flower sponge into Soft Blue and blot excess paint on paper towel. Referring to photo for placement, press sponge onto stool legs to paint flowers. Let dry. In same manner, paint leaves with Dusty Sage. Let dry.

4. Paint details on sponge-painted designs with liner brush, using Dusty Blue for flowers and Deep Sage for leaves. Let dry. Paint vines and tendrils, using liner brush and Deep Sage. Let dry. To paint dots on stool, dip cotton swab into Soft Fuchsia and dot on stool leg in desired positions. Let dry. Spray painted areas of stool with 1 or 2 coats of finish, letting dry between coats.

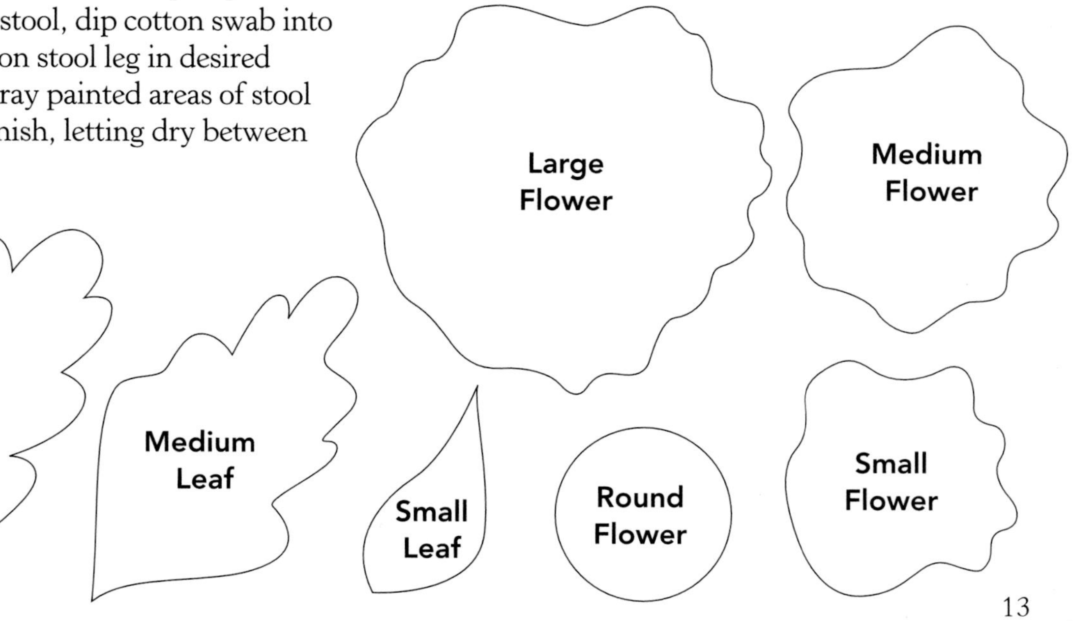

Resin Chair Update

Give your resin patio chair an expensive look with paper napkin appliqué.

Materials

- **For chair:** White resin chair
- Print paper napkins
- Aleene's Paper Napkin Appliqué Glue™
- Sponge paintbrush
- **For pad:** 2 (17") squares white-on-white print fabric
- 17" square thick batting
- Aleene's OK to Wash-It Glue™ or white thread
- Aleene's Premium-Coat™ Acrylic Paint in color to match napkin motif
- Waxed paper
- Aleene's Enhancers™ Textile Medium
- ½" square sponge piece
- 9 assorted buttons, thread, and 2 (32") lengths ¼"-wide ribbon in color to match napkin motif
- Clear spray polyurethane finish

Directions for chair

1. If needed, wash and dry chair. Cut motifs from napkins as desired. Remove bottom plies of napkin to leave cutouts 1-ply thick. Brush coat of Napkin Appliqué Glue on chair in desired position. Press cutout into glue. Gently brush top of cutout with coat of Napkin Appliqué Glue, being sure to seal edges with glue. Repeat to apply additional cutouts to chair as desired. Let dry.

2. Spray chair with 1 or 2 coats of finish, letting dry between coats.

Directions for pad

1. Wash and dry fabric; do not use fabric softener in washer or dryer. Round off 2 adjacent corners of each fabric square and batting square. With wrong sides facing and raw edges aligned, stack fabric pieces. Using ½" seam allowance, glue or stitch fabric pieces together around 3 sides. Let glue dry. Turn right side out and insert batting. Turn under ½" along opening and glue or stitch opening closed. Let glue dry.

2. Pour small puddle of paint onto waxed paper. Mix equal parts textile medium and paint. Dip dampened sponge piece into paint and blot excess paint on paper towel. Press sponge onto chair pad to paint squares about ⅜" apart above and below seam line of pad (see photo). Let dry.

3. Stitch 3 rows of 3 buttons each onto chair pad, pulling thread tightly to indent pad (see photo). For ties, glue 1" at center of each ribbon length to seam line near corners along rounded edge of pad. Let dry.

Floral Furnishing

Create a one-of-a-kind chest by stamping garlands of flowers and leaves on a thrift-store dresser.

Materials

- Dresser
- Furniture stripper (optional)
- Fine-grade sandpaper
- Tack cloth
- Flat white spray paint
- Aleene's Enhancers™ Clear Gel Medium
- Aleene's Premium-Coat™ Acrylic Paints: Yellow Ochre, Medium Red, True Red, Dusty Sage, Deep Sage, Burnt Umber, True Apricot
- Sponge paintbrush
- Fun Foam scraps
- Dry ballpoint pen
- Foam-core board scraps
- Aleene's Designer Tacky Glue™
- Aleene's Premium Designer Brushes™: shader, liner
- Cotton swab
- Clear spray polyurethane finish

Directions

1. Remove drawer pulls from dresser drawers. If needed, strip old paint and finish from dresser, drawers, and drawer pulls. Sand dresser, drawers, and drawer pulls. Wipe all pieces with tack cloth to remove any dust. Spray-paint each piece white to prime. Let dry.

2. Mix 2 parts clear gel medium with 1 part Yellow Ochre paint. Using sponge brush, apply uneven coat of mixture to each item to get antique stained effect (see photo). Let dry.

3. To make each foam stamp, transfer patterns to Fun Foam and cut 1 leaf A, 1 leaf B, 1 leaf C, 1 flower A, and 1 flower B. Using dry ballpoint pen, make indentations in each foam leaf where indicated on pattern. Cut 1 piece of foam core slightly larger than each foam piece. Center and glue 1 foam piece on each piece of foam core. Let dry.

4. To paint designs on dresser and drawers, brush desired color of paint on 1 stamp. Position stamp on dresser and press firmly, being sure all areas of stamp come in contact with dresser. Carefully lift stamp off dresser. Let dry. Referring to photo for placement, stamp additional designs on dresser and drawers. To get antique effect, do not apply fresh coat of paint to stamp before each printing. Paint flowers with Medium Red or True Red. Paint leaves with Dusty Sage, Deep Sage, and mixture of Dusty Sage and True Red or mixture of Dusty Sage and Burnt Umber as desired. Let dry.

5. Use liner brush to paint details on leaves, vines, stems, and tendrils with Deep Sage and Burnt Umber as desired. Let dry. To paint center on each flower A, dip cotton swab into True Apricot and dot on dresser and drawers. Let dry. Spray dresser, drawers, and drawer pulls with 1 or 2 coats of finish, letting dry between coats.

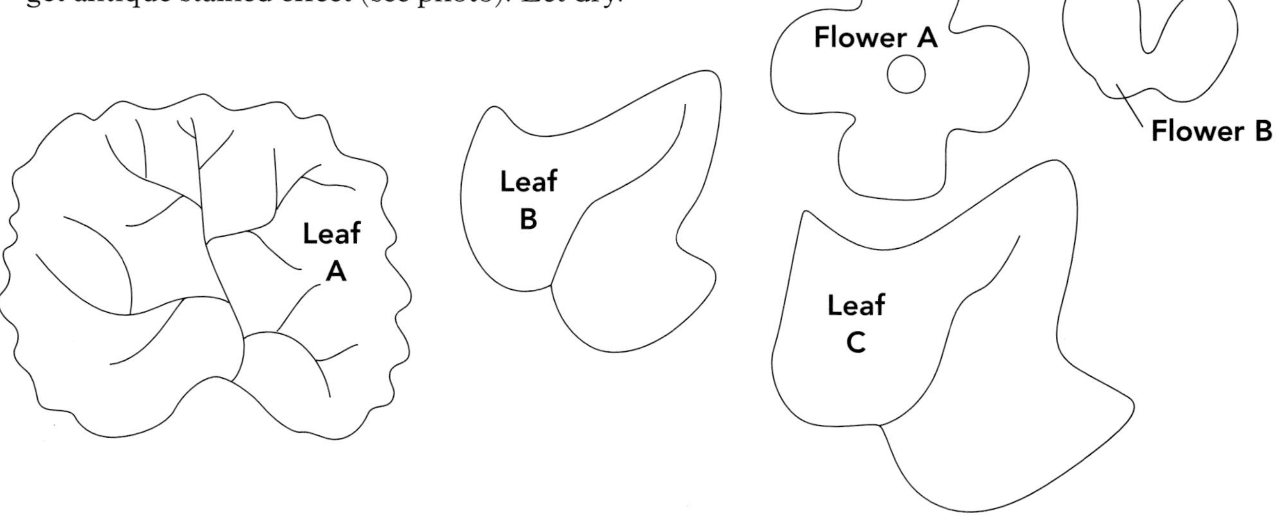

Daffodil Bouquets

These bright blooms are easy to make from a brown grocery bag and acrylic paints.

Materials

- **For 1 bouquet:** Plastic container
- Sandpaper
- Aleene's Premium-Coat™ Acrylic Paints: Deep Peach, True Yellow, True Apricot, Medium Yellow, White, Soft Sage, Dusty Sage, Deep Sage
- Aleene's Premium Designer Brushes™: shader, liner
- Block of Styrofoam to fit inside container
- Aleene's Tacky Glue™
- Brown grocery bag
- 3" square cardboard squeegee
- Scallop-edged scissors
- Craft knife
- 18-gauge florist's wire
- Green florist's tape
- Moss
- Wire-edged ribbon

Directions for 1 bouquet

1. Wash and dry container. Sand outside of container to roughen surface so that paint will adhere. Paint outside of container with 1 or 2 coats of Deep Peach, letting dry between coats. Glue foam inside container. Let dry.

2. For each daffodil, cut 2 (4½" x 6½") pieces and 1 (½" x 1¼") piece of brown bag. With edges aligned, glue 4½" x 6½" bag pieces together, using squeegee to apply thin coat of glue between layers. Transfer patterns on page 20 to layered bag and cut 1 petals and 1 trumpet. Trim curved edge of trumpet with scallop-edged scissors. Curve trumpet into cone, overlapping straight edges slightly, and glue. Let dry. Score petals along lines indicated on pattern, using craft knife. Bend petals piece along scored lines to add dimension (see photo). Overlap edges of slit and glue to form petals. Let dry.

3. For daffodil center, paint ½" x 1¼" bag piece True Yellow. Add shading with True Apricot. Let dry. Fringe 1 short end. Cut florist's wire to desired length for daffodil stem. Bend 1 end of wire to form small loop. Wrap and glue unfringed end of daffodil center around wire loop. Let dry. Referring to photos for color placement, paint petals and trumpet. Let dry.

4. Insert free end of stem wire through hole in trumpet and then through hole in petals, pushing trumpet and petals up to daffodil center. Glue daffodil pieces together to secure. Let dry. Beginning at base of petals, wrap florist's tape around entire length of stem wire. Paint tape Soft Sage as desired. Let dry.

5. For each leaf, cut 3 pieces of brown bag, ½" larger all around than desired leaf pattern on page 20. Cut 1 length of florist's wire 1½" longer than wire placement line on desired leaf pattern. With edges aligned, glue 2 bag pieces together, using squeegee to apply thin coat of glue between layers. With edges aligned and wire sandwiched between layers where indicated on pattern, glue remaining bag piece to 1 side of layered bag. While glue is still wet, transfer pattern to layered bag and cut out leaf; do not cut through wire. With wire at back of leaf, shape leaf as desired. Let dry.

6. Paint leaf Soft Sage, Dusty Sage, and Deep Sage to get desired effect (see photo). Let dry.

7. Make desired number of daffodils and leaves for bouquet. Dip end of wire of each piece into glue and push into foam to create bouquet. Glue moss to cover foam. Let dry. Tie ribbon in bow around container.

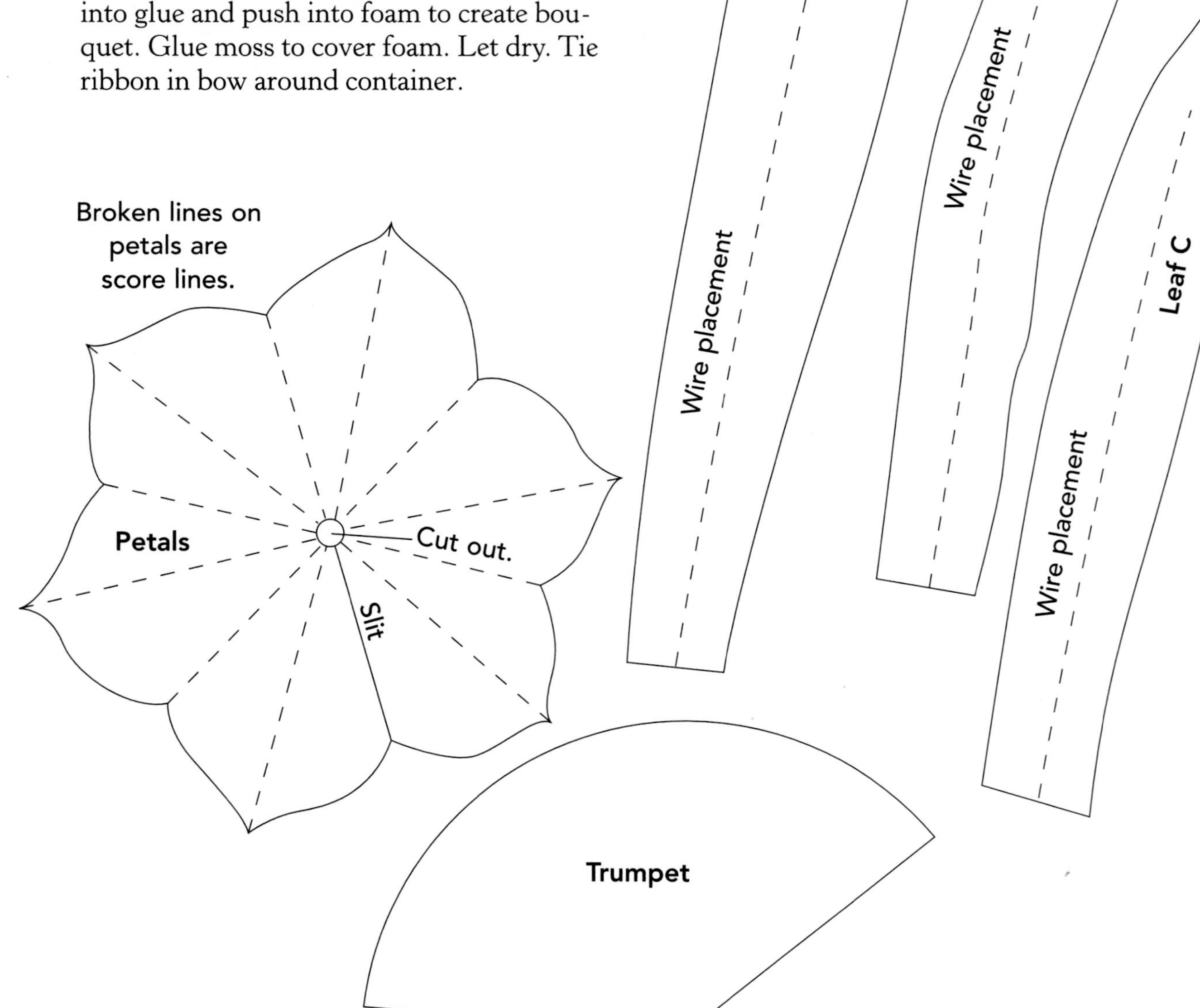

Playtime Table & Chairs

Paint a pair of chairs and a small trunk in vibrant colors for your child's room.

Materials

- 1 small square trunk
- 2 small chairs
- Flat white spray paint
- Aleene's Premium-Coat™ Acrylic Paints: True Lavender, Medium Turquoise, True Lime, True Yellow, Medium Yellow, True Turquoise, Medium Violet, Medium Blue, Medium Lime, Medium Fuchsia, True Violet
- Sponge paintbrush
- Aleene's Premium Designer Brushes™: shader, liner
- Pop-up craft sponges
- Fun Foam: scraps, 1 sheet each of 2 colors
- 3 pencils with erasers
- Cotton swabs
- Aleene's Designer Tacky Glue™
- Clear spray polyurethane finish
- Assorted colors dimensional paints (optional)

Directions

1. Spray-paint trunk and each chair white to prime. Let dry. **For trunk,** paint surface of trunk True Lavender. Let dry. Paint brass fittings on trunk Medium Turquoise. Let dry. Paint heads of rivets on brass fittings True Lime and True Yellow as desired. Let dry. **For each chair,** sketch grid of 2¾" squares on seat. Paint squares of grid, alternating paint colors as desired. Paint feet and back Medium Yellow and rim of seat and remainder of chair True Turquoise. Let dry. Referring to photo, paint 1"-wide vertical stripes on chair back with Medium Violet, Medium Blue, and Medium Lime. Paint wavy lines along each edge of each stripe, using liner brush and Medium Fuchsia. Let dry.

2. **For trunk,** center and sketch 3 x 3 grid of 3¼" squares on top of trunk. Paint each corner square Medium Lime, center square Medium Yellow, squares to left and right of center square Medium Violet, and squares at top and bottom of center square Medium Fuchsia. Let dry. Paint wavy lines along edges of squares, using liner brush and True Violet. Let dry.

Make foam stamps to print the hearts and the stars on the chair and then paint the squiggles, the swirls, and the other designs freehand. You may want to practice the freehand designs on scrap paper before painting them on the chair.

3. For each chair, transfer patterns and cut 1 rectangle from pop-up craft sponge and 1 small star and 1 small heart from Fun Foam scraps. Dip sponge shape into water to expand and wring out excess water. Dip sponge into Medium Yellow and blot excess paint on paper towel. Press sponge onto chair to paint rectangles about 1" apart around rim of seat. Let dry. Glue each foam shape to 1 pencil eraser. Let dry.

4. For each item, referring to photos, paint swirls and other designs on trunk and each chair seat, using liner brush and desired colors. To paint stars and hearts on each chair seat, dip each foam shape into desired color of paint and press onto chair. Let dry. To paint dots, dip cotton swab, handle of brush, or remaining pencil eraser into desired color of paint and dot on trunk or chair. Let dry. Spray trunk and each chair with 1 or 2 coats of finish, letting dry between coats.

5. For tic-tac-toe game pieces, transfer patterns to Fun Foam and cut 4 large hearts from 1 color and 4 large stars from remaining color. If desired, decorate 1 side of each shape with dimensional paints. Let dry.

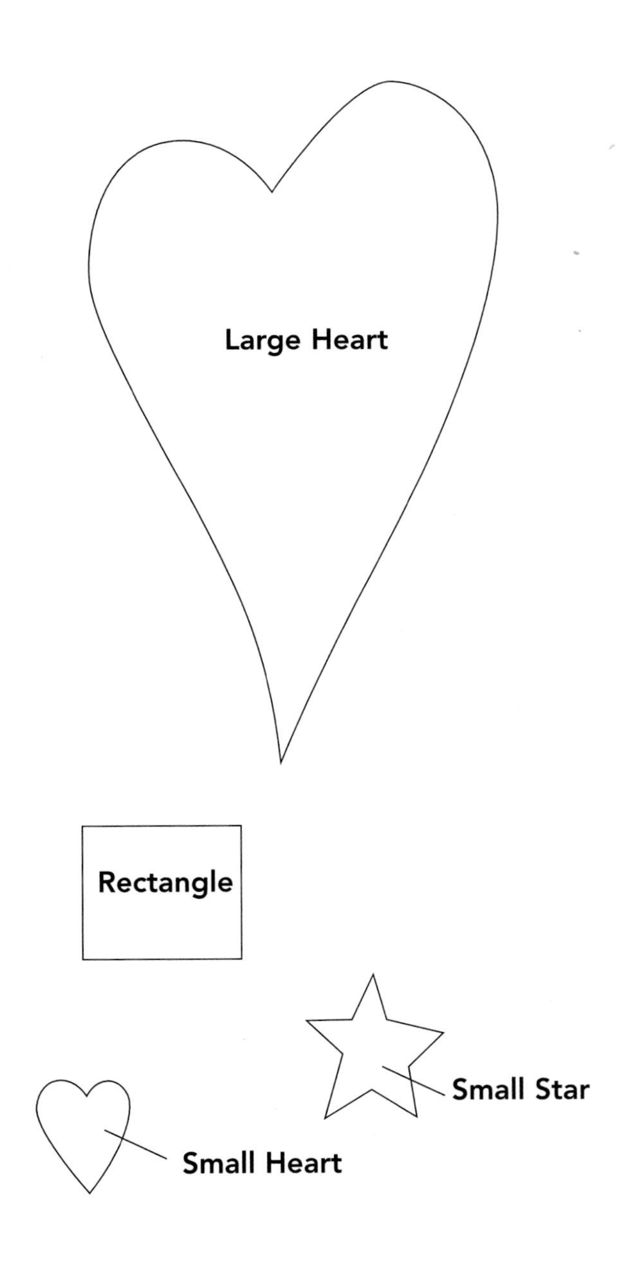

Large Star

An Heirloom Look

Gather a few inexpensive materials and some metallic paint to turn ordinary frames into elegant decor.

Gilded Ivy Frame

Materials

- Wooden picture frame
- Fine-grade sandpaper (optional)
- Tack cloth
- Spray paints: flat white, silver, gold
- 12 silk ivy leaves in assorted sizes
- Aleene's 3-D Foiling Glue™
- Aleene's Crafting Foil™: silver, gold
- Aleene's Designer Tacky Glue™

Directions

1. Sand frame to remove old paint, if needed. Wipe frame with tack cloth to remove any dust. Spray-paint entire frame white to prime. Spray-paint entire frame silver and right side of each leaf gold. Let dry.

2. Referring to Diagram on page 5, make tape tip for bottle of 3-D Foiling Glue. Outline each leaf and add veins with lines of 3-D Foiling Glue. Let dry. (Glue will be opaque and sticky when dry. Glue must be thoroughly dry before foil is applied.) To apply foil, lay silver foil dull side down on top of glue lines. Using finger, gently but firmly press foil onto glue, completely covering glue with foil. Peel away foil paper. If any part of glue is not covered, reapply foil as needed.

3. Glue leaves to frame as desired, shaping leaves to add dimension and using Designer Tacky Glue. Let dry. Apply lines of 3-D Foiling Glue to frame for leaf stems and tendrils. Apply gold foil to glue lines as before.

Braid Frame

Materials

- Masking tape
- 5" x 7" acrylic frame
- Gold spray paint
- Gold-and-black braid: 2 (5") lengths, 2 (8") lengths
- Aleene's Designer Tacky Glue™

Directions

Cut several 4" lengths of masking tape. Center and press tape lengths, overlapping side edges slightly, on right side of frame to make 2½" x 4" rectangle. Be sure all edges of tape are firmly adhered to frame to keep paint from seeping under tape. Spray-paint frame gold. Let dry. Remove masking tape. Glue braid lengths to frame along edges of unpainted rectangle. Let dry.

You'll be surprised how easy it is to make this lovely frame.

Ribbons & Lace

Search flea markets and garage sales for vintage lace tablecloths. You'll be using only selected sections of the fabric, so don't worry about a few stains or holes.

Materials

- **For each:** Lace tablecloth
- Aleene's OK to Wash-It Glue™
- Assorted colors 1"-wide sheer ribbon
- **For pillow:** 2 (14") squares fabric
- Thread
- 14" square pillow or pillow form
- Assorted colors 2"-wide sheer ribbon

Directions for curtain

1. To determine desired width and length of curtain, measure width of window inside molding and length of window from midpoint to bottom. Add 1" for hems to width measurement. Add 2½" for casing to length measurement. Referring to Curtain Diagram, cut 1 corner from tablecloth for curtain. Turn under ½" along each raw side edge of curtain and glue for hem. Turn under 2½" along top raw edge of curtain and glue for casing. Let dry.

2. Cut several 18" lengths from assorted colors of 1"-wide ribbon. Thread each ribbon through lace where desired and tie ends in bow on right side of curtain.

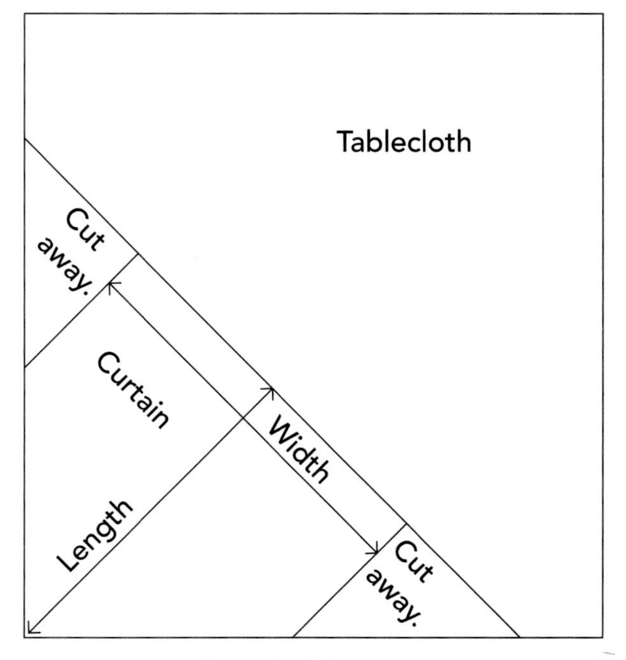

Curtain Diagram

Directions for pillow

1. Cut 1 (14") square from tablecloth. With edges aligned, stack 1 fabric square (right side up), lace square (right side up), and remaining fabric square (wrong side up). Using ½" seam allowance, stitch squares together around 3 sides. Turn pillow cover right side out. Insert pillow or pillow form. Turn under ½" along opening and stitch opening closed.

2. Cut 1 (18") length of 1"-wide ribbon from each of 4 colors. Tie each ribbon in bow. Glue 1 bow on pillow front at each corner. Cut 1 (40") length of 1"-wide ribbon. Form 6 (2½") loops with ribbon and secure center of bow with thread. Center and glue bow on pillow front.

3. Cut 1 (15") length of 2"-wide ribbon from each of 3 colors. Referring to Flower Diagram, fold down top corner at 1 end of 1 ribbon length. Roll folded end of ribbon for about ¾" to form center of flower. Beginning at rolled end, run gathering thread along bottom edge of ribbon length. Pull thread to gather ribbon, forming flower. Secure thread. Repeat with each remaining 15" ribbon length. Glue ribbon flowers on top of multi-looped bow on pillow. Let dry.

Flower Diagram

Painted Pansy Mat

Make a foam stamp to paint this pansy design on the back of a piece of vinyl floor covering.

Materials
- Sponge roller paintbrush
- Aleene's Premium-Coat™ Acrylic Paints: Ivory, Light Green, Medium Green, Deep Violet, True Violet, Medium Violet, Deep Fuchsia, True Fuchsia, Medium Fuchsia, True Yellow, Medium Yellow, True Apricot, Medium Apricot, True Orange, Black, True Green, Deep Green
- 20" x 31" piece vinyl floor covering
- Fun Foam scraps
- Foam-core board scraps
- Aleene's Designer Tacky Glue™
- Aleene's Premium Designer Brushes™: liner, shader
- Clear spray polyurethane finish

Directions

1. Use sponge roller to apply 1 or 2 coats of Ivory to wrong side of vinyl, letting dry between coats. Paint 1 (2" x 16") band across each short end of vinyl with Light Green, centering band on width of vinyl and leaving 2" unpainted at each corner. Let dry. In same manner, paint 1 (2" x 27") band across each long edge of vinyl with Light Green. Let dry. Referring to photo, paint wavy line along edge of each Light Green band, using liner brush and Medium Green. Let dry.

Mix and match paint colors to paint a field of pansies on your mat. Nature combines colors in unusual ways so don't be afraid to experiment with a few wild combinations of your own.

2. To make each stamp, transfer patterns on page 30 to Fun Foam and cut 1 of each pansy petal and 1 pansy leaf. Cut 1 (5¼") square and 1 (3" x 5") piece of foam core. Referring to pattern for positioning, center and glue foam pansy petals on 5¼" square of foam core. Center and glue foam pansy leaf on 3" x 5" foam core. Let dry.

3. To paint each pansy, brush desired colors of paint onto pansy stamp. Position stamp on vinyl and press firmly, being sure all areas of stamp come in contact with vinyl. Carefully lift stamp off vinyl. Let dry. Repeat to stamp additional pansies on vinyl, applying fresh coat of paints to stamp before each printing. To apply different paint colors to stamp, wipe stamp with damp paper towel, let dry, and then apply new colors. Use brushes and desired colors of paint to add shading to each pansy. Outline pansy petals and add details, using liner brush and desired colors. Let dry.

4. To paint each whole leaf, brush True Green paint on leaf stamp. Refer to Step 3 to stamp leaf on vinyl. For each partial leaf, let stamp dry and then apply True Green to desired area of stamp for partial leaf (see photo). Outline each leaf, paint center vein on each leaf, and paint tendrils, using liner brush and Deep Green. Let dry. Spray mat with 1 or 2 coats of finish, letting dry between coats.

Painted Pansy Mat patterns

Directions are on page 29.

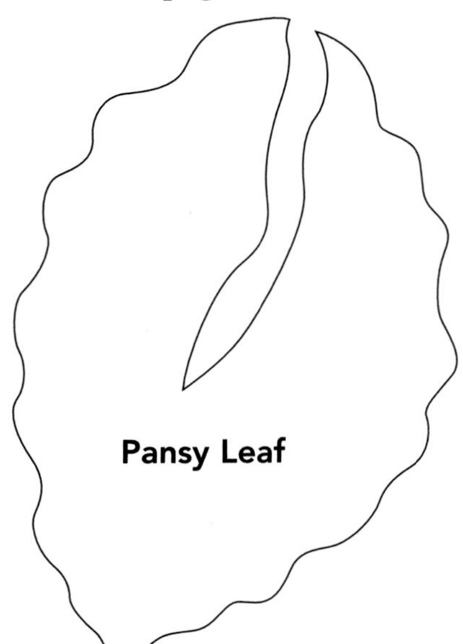

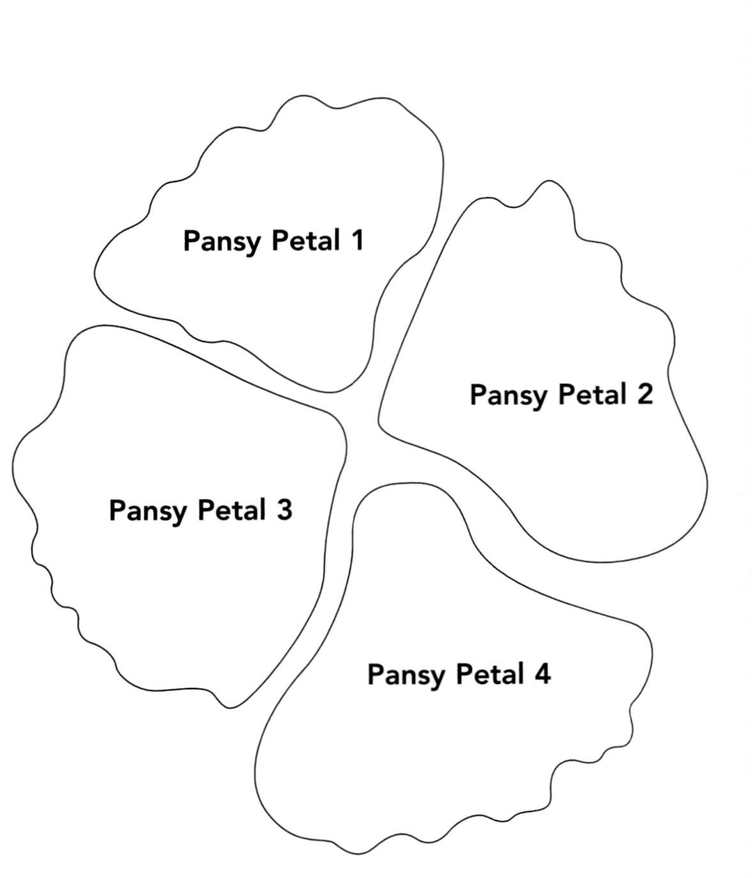

Sponge-painted Window Shade patterns

Directions are on page 32.

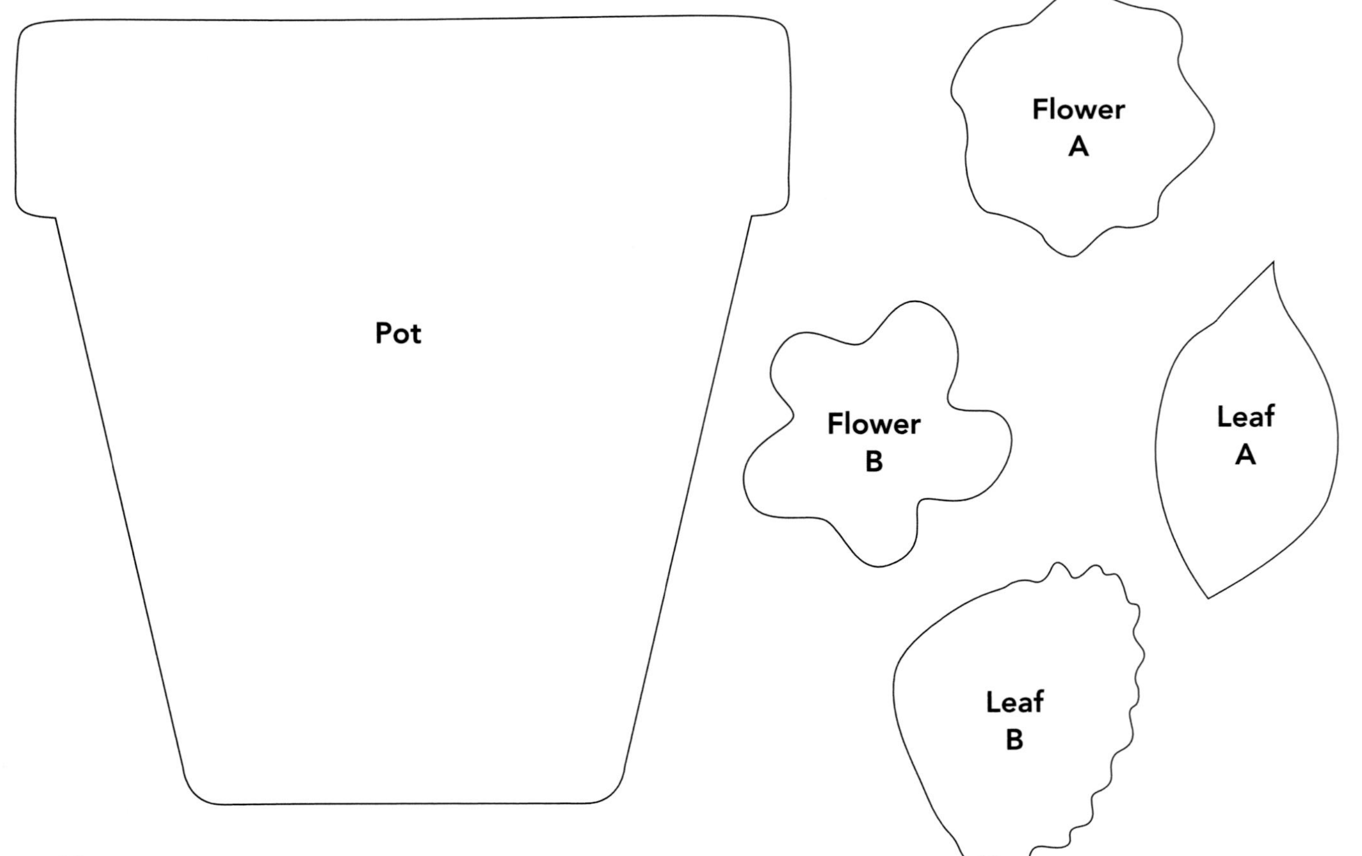

Sponge-painted Window Shade

Create an enchanting window treatment when you sponge-paint flowerpots on a plain roller shade.

Materials

- Vinyl roller shade
- Pop-up craft sponges
- Aleene's Premium-Coat™ Acrylic Paints: Deep Mauve, Dusty Beige, Light Fuchsia, Dark Fuchsia, Medium Yellow, Medium Apricot, True Poppy, Dusty Sage, Deep Sage
- Waxed paper
- Natural sea sponge
- Small sponge paintbrush
- Aleene's Premium Designer Brush™: liner
- Clear spray sealer (optional)
- 24" length 2"-wide ecru pregathered lace trim
- Aleene's Designer Tacky Glue™

Directions

1. Referring to photo, lightly sketch ¾"-wide strips on shade for windowpanes, centering vertical strip on width of shade and positioning horizontal strip about 16" from bottom of shade. With bottom of each pot about 1¾" from bottom of shade and top of pots spaced about 3" apart, transfer pot pattern on page 30 to shade 3 times. Transfer patterns on page 30 to pop-up craft sponges and cut 1 flower A, 1 flower B, 1 leaf A, and 1 leaf B. Cut 1 (⅞") square from pop-up craft sponge. Dip each sponge shape into water to expand and wring out excess water.

2. Pour separate puddles of paint onto waxed paper. To paint each pot, dip dampened natural sea sponge into Deep Mauve and press sponge onto shade within marked line of each pot. Let dry. Sponge-paint pot with Dusty Beige just below rim to add shading. To paint windowpane strips, dip dampened sponge brush into Dusty Beige and press onto shade within marked lines. Let dry. Sponge-paint edges of each strip, using tip of sponge brush and Deep Mauve. Let dry.

3. To paint flowers and leaves, dip 1 dampened sponge shape into desired color of paint and blot excess paint on paper towel. Press sponge shape onto shade as desired. Repeat to paint additional flowers and leaves on shade. Let dry. Rinse each sponge thoroughly before dipping into different paint color. To get shaded effect on flowers, dip part of sponge into 1 paint color and then dip remainder of sponge into another paint color. Blot excess paint on paper towel, blending paint colors to get desired effect.

4. Paint details on flowers and leaves, using liner brush and desired colors of paint. Let dry. Dip dampened ⅞" square sponge into True Poppy and Dark Fuchsia paints and blot excess paint on paper towel, blending colors slightly. Press sponge square onto shade to paint squares about ⅞" apart along bottom edge of shade. Let dry.

5. If desired, spray shade with sealer. Let dry. Glue bound edge of lace to wrong side of shade along bottom edge so that lace extends beyond edge of shade. Let dry.

Jar-o'-Buttons Lamp

A purchased lamp kit means you don't have to be an electrician to create this charming lamp.

Materials
- 6" length cardboard tube
- 2-quart canning jar and jar-lid lamp kit
- Buttons
- Aleene's Satin Sheen Twisted Ribbon™: off-white
- Lampshade
- Button print fabric (See Step 2.)
- Aleene's Tacky Glue™
- Pregathered lace trim to match fabric (See Step 3.)

Directions
1. Center and place cardboard tube inside jar. Fill jar around tube with buttons. Screw lamp kit onto jar. Cut 1 (26") length of twisted ribbon. Untwist ribbon. Tear ribbon into narrow lengthwise strips. Handling several narrow strips as 1, tie strips in bow around top of jar.

2. To make shade pattern, starting at seam, roll shade on large sheet of paper and mark bottom edge of shade as you roll. Realign shade and repeat to mark top edge. Draw line connecting top and bottom lines at each end of pattern. Cut out pattern. Transfer pattern to fabric and cut out, adding 1" all around. To cover shade, center shade on width of fabric. Starting at seam, apply glue to shade and gently roll shade on fabric. Continue around shade, smoothing fabric as you go. Overlap ends of fabric, turn top end under ½", and glue. Let dry. Fold top and bottom edges of fabric to inside of shade and glue, clipping curves as needed. Let dry.

3. Measure around top and bottom edges of shade and cut 1 length each of lace trim to these measurements. Starting at seam, glue bound edge of lace trim around corresponding edge on wrong side of shade so that lace extends beyond shade. Let dry. Glue 1 row of buttons around bottom edge of shade. Glue several buttons to shade as desired. Let dry.

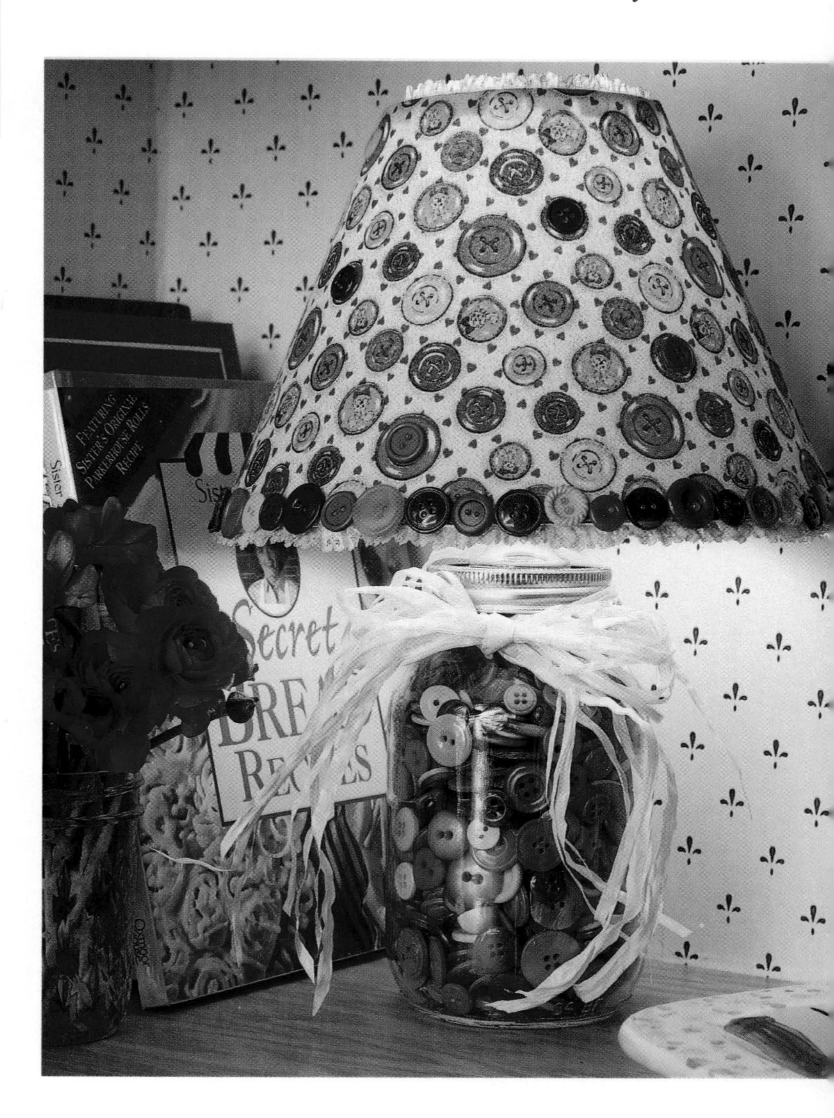

TACK

Decoupaged Trays

For these decorative trays, glue print fabric or a paper picture onto a plastic or cardboard tray.

Materials

- **For each:** Plastic or cardboard tray
- Sponge paintbrush
- Aleene's Instant Decoupage™ Glue
- **For picture tray:** Aleene's Premium-Coat™ Acrylic Paints: Black, True Grey, Deep Blush, Dusty Green
- Aleene's Decoupage Print™: Farm House
- Pop-up craft sponges
- Waxed paper
- Cotton swab
- **For fabric tray:** 2 complementary print fabrics (See Step 1).

Directions for picture tray

1. If needed, wash and dry tray. Paint tray with 1 or 2 coats of Black, letting dry between coats. If needed, trim print to fit tray. Brush coat of glue on inside bottom of tray where print will be placed. Brush coat of glue on wrong side of print. Glue print in place on tray, pressing out any air bubbles. Brush top of print with glue. Let dry.

2. Transfer patterns to pop-up craft sponges and cut 1 house, 1 roof, and 1 tree. Dip each sponge shape into water to expand and wring out excess water. Pour separate puddles of paint onto waxed paper. Dip house sponge into True Grey and blot excess paint on paper towel. Referring to photo for placement, press sponge onto tray to paint houses. Let dry. In same manner, paint 1 roof on each house with Deep Blush and paint trees with Dusty Green. Let dry. Dip cotton swab into Deep Blush and press onto tray to paint dots around edge of print. Let dry.

3. Brush 1 or 2 coats of glue on entire surface of tray, letting dry between coats.

Directions for fabric tray

1. If needed, wash and dry tray. To determine width and length of print fabric strip needed for rim of tray, measure depth of tray rim from bottom of tray to outer edge. Measure circumference of tray. Add 1" to each measurement. Cut strip to these measurements from 1 print fabric. Measure dimensions of inside bottom of tray to determine amount of fabric needed. Cut fabric piece to these measurements from other print fabric.

2. Brush coat of glue on top of tray rim. Press fabric strip into glue around rim of tray so that 1 long edge extends beyond edge of rim far enough to reach bottom of tray. Press out any air bubbles. Overlap short ends of fabric strip, turn top end under ½", and glue. Brush coat of glue on bottom of tray rim. Press fabric into glue, pressing out any air bubbles and clipping fabric every 1½". Brush coat of glue on inside bottom of tray. Press remaining fabric piece into glue, pressing out any air bubbles.

3. Brush 1 or 2 coats of glue on entire surface of tray, letting dry between coats.

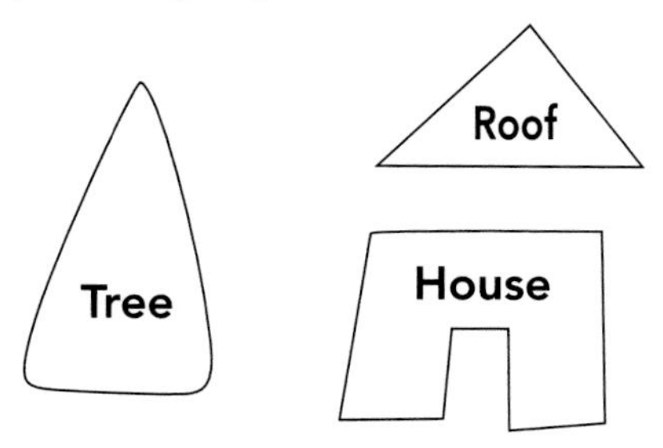

Teapot Lamp

Start this project with a small purchased lamp. Glue on a wooden spout and handle to form a teapot.

Materials

- 4" x 7" piece ¼"-thick wood
- Saw
- Fine-grade sandpaper
- Tack cloth
- Lamp with ball-shaped base
- Aleene's Premium-Coat™ Acrylic Paints: Black, Ivory, Medium Lavender, Medium Violet, Medium Green, True Lavender, True Violet, Holiday Green, Medium Fuchsia, Medium Yellow, True Apricot
- Aleene's Premium Designer Brushes™: shader, liner
- Aleene's Tacky Glue™
- Pop-up craft sponges
- Waxed paper
- Clear spray sealer
- Lampshade
- Black-and-white checked fabric (See Step 4.)
- Pregathered lace trim (See Step 5.)
- Decorative flat braid (See Step 5.)
- 20" length 1"-wide sheer ribbon
- Wire-edged ribbons: 1 (15") length 1⅜"-wide variegated purple, 2 (4") lengths 1⅜"-wide variegated green
- Thread
- 1 (½") button

Directions

1. Transfer patterns on page 38 to wood and cut 1 spout and 1 handle. Sand wood pieces smooth. Wipe wood pieces with tack cloth to remove any dust. Paint spout, handle, and lamp base with 1 or 2 coats of Black, letting dry between coats. Glue spout and handle to opposite sides of lamp base. Let dry.

2. Transfer patterns on page 38 to pop-up craft sponges and cut 1 square, 1 flower, and 1 leaf. Dip each sponge shape into water to expand and wring out excess water. Pour separate puddles of paint onto waxed paper. Dip square sponge into Ivory and blot excess paint on paper towel. Referring to photo for placement, press sponge onto lamp to paint row of squares around top and bottom of base. Let dry. In same manner, paint flowers with Medium Lavender and Medium Violet and leaves with Medium Green. Rinse each sponge thoroughly before dipping into different paint color. Paint True Lavender and True Violet details on flowers and Holiday Green details on leaves, using liner brush. Let dry.

3. Referring to photo and using liner brush, paint tiny Ivory and Medium Fuchsia flowers and Medium Green leaves and vines on lamp, spout, and handle. Let dry. Dip handle of 1 brush into Medium Yellow and press onto lamp to paint center of each sponge-painted flower. In same manner, paint 1 True Apricot center on each tiny flower. Let dry. Spray lamp with 1 or 2 coats of sealer, letting dry between coats.

If your lamp base is larger than 6" in diameter, use a photocopier to enlarge all the patterns to get the best effect with your finished project. If you are unable to find a lamp with a ball-shaped base, omit the spout and the handle and use the teapot and teacup patterns on page 41 to sponge-paint motifs on the lamp base.

Essentials
of Classic
Italian

4. To make shade pattern, starting at seam, roll shade on large sheet of paper and mark bottom edge of shade as you roll. Realign shade and repeat to mark top edge. Draw line connecting top and bottom lines at each end of pattern. Cut out pattern. Transfer pattern to fabric and cut out, adding 1" all around. To cover shade, center shade on width of fabric. Starting at seam, apply glue to shade and gently roll shade on fabric. Continue around shade, smoothing fabric as you go. Overlap ends of fabric, turn top end under ½", and glue. Let dry. Fold top and bottom edges of fabric to inside of shade and glue, clipping curves as needed. Let dry.

5. Measure around top and bottom edges of shade and cut 1 length each of lace trim and flat braid. Starting at seam, glue bound edge of each piece of lace trim around corresponding edge on right side of shade so that lace extends beyond shade. Glue each piece of flat braid around corresponding edge on right side of shade, covering bound edge of lace. Let dry.

6. Tie sheer ribbon in bow. Glue bow to shade. Let dry. Referring to Flower Diagram, measure and mark 3" sections on purple ribbon. Run gathering thread along ribbon as shown on Diagram. Pull thread to gather ribbon into flower and secure thread. Referring to Leaf Diagram, fold down 1 end of each green ribbon length to form right angle; then fold left end of ribbon to back along line indicated to form point. Pinch ribbon ends together to shape bottom of leaf. Glue ribbon leaves and flower on top of bow on shade. Glue button in place for flower center. Let dry.

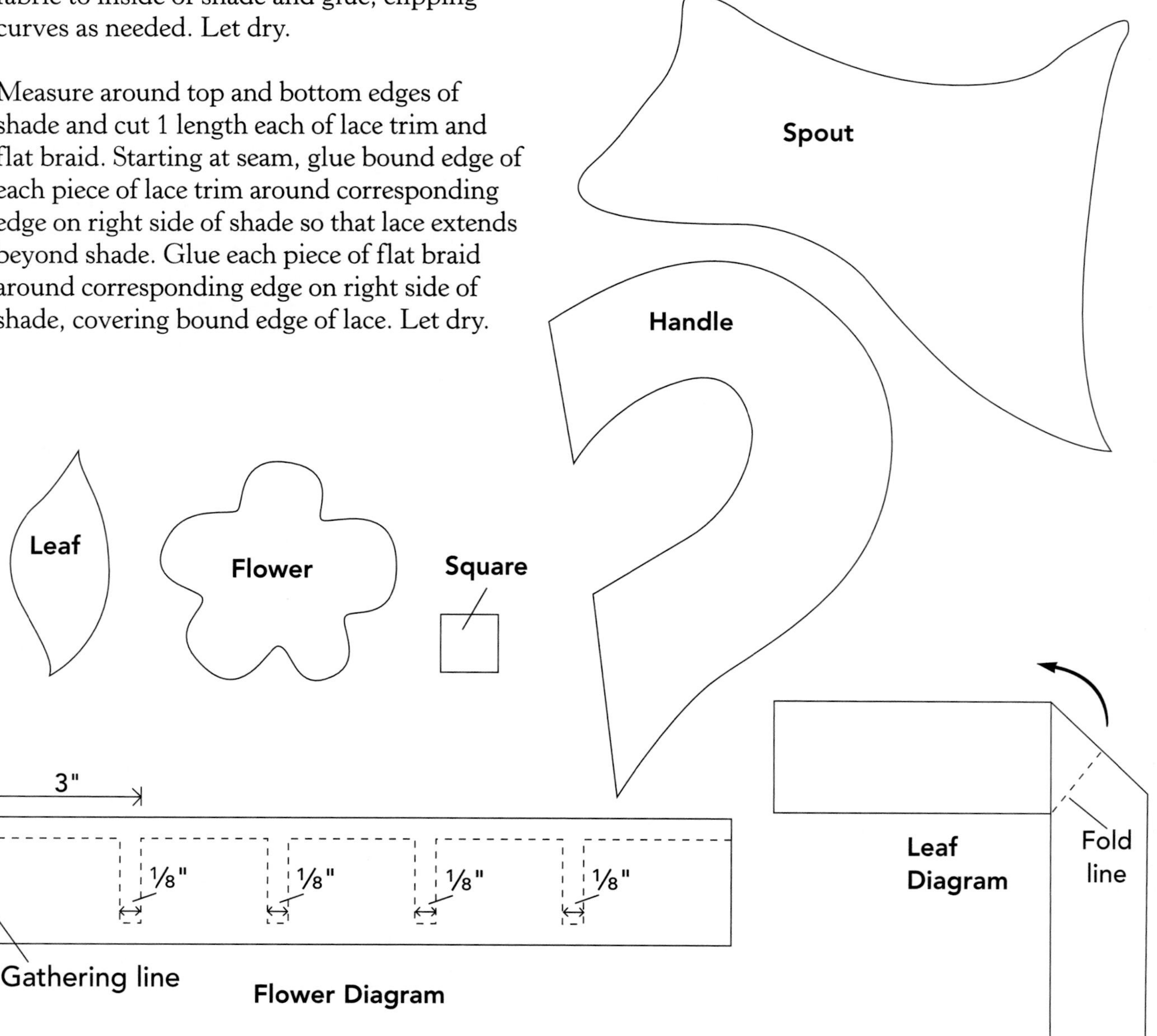

Pretty-as-a-Picture

Paint garlands of flowers on a picture mat to add a fancy touch to a plain purchased frame.

Materials
- Fun Foam scraps
- 2 pencils with erasers
- Aleene's Designer Tacky Glue™
- Aleene's Premium-Coat™ Acrylic Paints: Medium Fuchsia, Dusty Sage, True Fuchsia, Deep Sage, Medium Violet, Medium Yellow
- Waxed paper
- Purchased picture mat to fit desired frame
- Aleene's Premium Designer Brush™: liner
- Toothpicks

Directions
1. Transfer patterns to Fun Foam and cut 1 flower and 1 leaf. Glue 1 foam piece to each pencil eraser. Let dry. Pour separate puddles of Medium Fuchsia and Dusty Sage onto waxed paper. Dip foam flower into Medium Fuchsia and press onto mat to paint flowers. In same manner, stamp Dusty Sage leaves onto mat. Let dry. Paint True Fuchsia details on flowers and Deep Sage vines and details on leaves, using liner brush. Let dry.

2. Pour separate puddles of Medium Violet and True Yellow onto waxed paper. To paint tiny dot flowers on mat, dip 1 toothpick into Medium Violet and press onto mat. Dip another toothpick into Medium Yellow and press onto mat to paint center of each tiny dot flower. Let dry.

Teatime Tray

Choose colors to match your teapot and teacups when you paint a tray like this one.

Materials

- Tray
- Flat white spray paint
- Aleene's Premium-Coat™ Acrylic Paints: Light Blue, Light Turquoise, Light Violet, Light Fuchsia, Light Lime, Medium Turquoise, Medium Violet, Medium Fuchsia, Medium Lime, Medium Yellow
- Sponge paintbrush
- Pop-up craft sponges
- Waxed paper
- Aleene's Premium Designer Brush™: liner
- Toothpick
- Clear spray sealer

Directions

1. If needed, wash and dry tray. Spray-paint tray white to prime. Paint tray with 1 or 2 coats of Light Blue for base coat, using sponge brush and letting dry between coats. Transfer patterns to pop-up craft sponges and cut 1 teapot, 1 teacup, 1 large rose, 1 small rose, 1 large leaf, 1 small leaf, and 1 heart. Dip each sponge shape into water to expand and wring out excess water.

2. Pour separate puddles of paint onto waxed paper. Dip teapot sponge into Light Turquoise and blot excess paint on paper towel. Referring to photo for placement, press sponge onto tray to paint 4 teapots. Let dry. In same manner, paint 4 teacups with Light Violet; 4 teacups, large roses, small roses, and hearts with Light Fuchsia; and large leaves and small leaves with Light Lime. Let dry. Rinse each sponge thoroughly before dipping into different paint color.

3. Paint details on sponge-painted designs with liner brush, using colors as follows: Medium Turquoise for teapots; Medium Violet for Light Violet teacups; Medium Fuchsia for Light Fuchsia teacups, large roses, and small roses; and Medium Lime for large leaves and small leaves. To paint tiny dots around edge of each heart, dip toothpick into Medium Yellow and press onto tray. For larger dots on tray, dip handle of liner brush into Medium Yellow and press onto tray. Let dry. Paint vines, using liner brush and Medium Lime. Let dry. Spray tray with 1 or 2 coats of sealer, letting dry between coats.

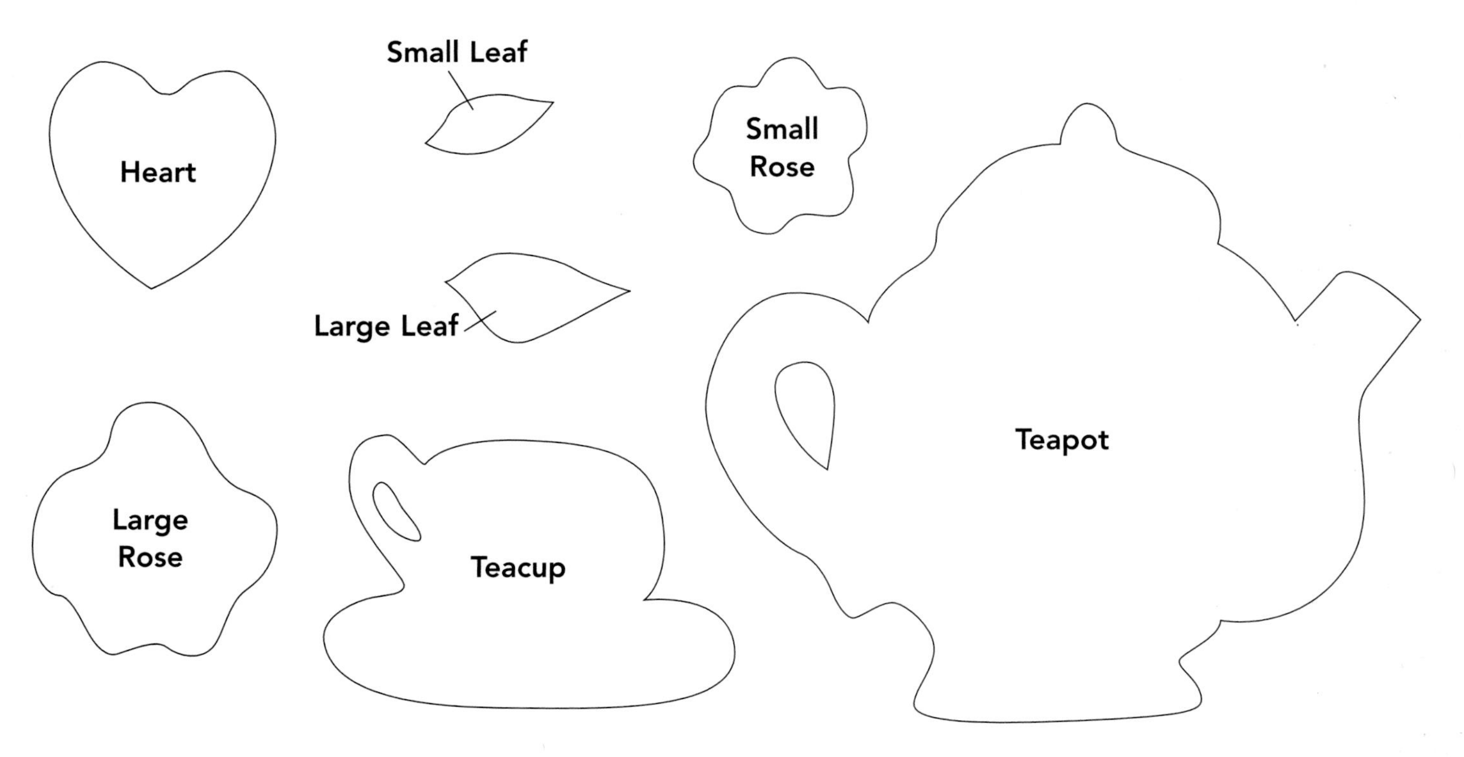

Throw-Pillow Embellishments

Use doilies, buttons, and tasseled trims to give new life to old pillows.

Materials

- **For each:** Throw pillow
- Aleene's OK to Wash-It Glue™
- **For diamond pillow:** Fabric square to match pillow (See Step 1.)
- Foam-core board work surface
- Waxed paper
- Square paper doily to fit fabric square
- Silver spray paint
- Aleene's Fusible Web™
- Small crocheted doily
- Decorative button
- Tassel
- Trim with fringe (See Step 2.)
- **For heart pillow:** Heart-shaped crocheted doily
- Assorted decorative buttons
- Trim with tassels (See directions.)

Directions for diamond pillow

1. Cut fabric square to fit pillow front when placed on point (see photos). Cover foam-core board work surface with waxed paper. Lay fabric square right side up on waxed paper. Center paper doily on right side of fabric square. Pin doily and fabric to foam core by sticking several pins straight down through all layers. Spray-paint fabric square silver. Let dry. Remove and discard paper doily.

2. Fuse web onto wrong side of fabric square. Place fabric square on point on pillow front and fuse in place (see photos). Center and glue crocheted doily on fabric square. Glue decorative button on top of doily, catching top of tassel under button. Let dry. Glue trim around edge of fabric square. Let dry.

Directions for heart pillow

Center and glue doily on pillow front. Glue decorative buttons to doily as desired. Let dry. Measure circumference of pillow and cut 1 length of trim to that measurement. Glue trim around pillow along seam. Let dry.

To paint a lacy design on fabric, lay a paper doily on solid-colored fabric and then spray-paint the fabric with a contrasting color of paint. Remove the paper doily to reveal the painted design. Use this technique to give a fresh look to cloth napkins or place mats for your dinner table or to decorate a set of chair pads for your kitchen.

Holiday Magic

Decorating for the holidays doesn't have to mean spending a lot of money. With the designs in these pages, you can make great-looking decorations without going broke. Get everyone into the spirit of the season—let your family help make projects.

Champagne-Cork Characters

Dress up champagne corks with paints, fabrics, and trims for these festive ornaments.

Materials

- **For each:** Aleene's Enhancers™ All-Purpose Primer
- 1 champagne cork (not plastic)
- Aleene's Premium Designer Brush™: shader
- Toothpicks
- Aleene's Designer Tacky Glue™
- 1 (6") length gold metallic thread
- **For Santa:** Aleene's Premium-Coat™ Acrylic Paints: Holiday Red, Blush, Black
- Red fabric scrap
- Felt scraps: white, black
- Gold paper scrap
- **For snowman:** Aleene's Premium-Coat™ Acrylic Paints: White, Black
- Orange dimensional paint
- Fine-tip permanent black marker
- 1 (¼" x 4¼") print fabric scrap
- Black paper scrap
- **For angel:** Aleene's Premium-Coat™ Acrylic Paints: Gold, Blush, Black
- 1"-diameter wooden bead
- Aleene's Premium Designer Brush™: liner
- White yarn
- Red embroidery floss
- 8" length ¾"-wide gold-and-white ribbon

Directions for Santa

1. Apply 1 coat of primer to cork. Let dry. Paint cork Holiday Red. Let dry. Paint ¾"-wide and ½"-high face just below edge on small end of cork with Blush. Let dry. Dip toothpick into Black and dot on face for eyes. Dip another toothpick into Holiday Red and dot on face for nose. Let dry.

2. Transfer patterns and cut 1 hat from red fabric and 1 beard and 1 mustache from white felt. Cut 1 (¼" x 3") strip for hat trim from remaining white felt. Cut 1 (¼" x 4¼") strip from black felt. Cut 1 (¼") square from gold paper for buckle. Glue beard and mustache on cork. Wrap and glue black felt strip around cork for belt. Glue buckle on belt. Let dry.

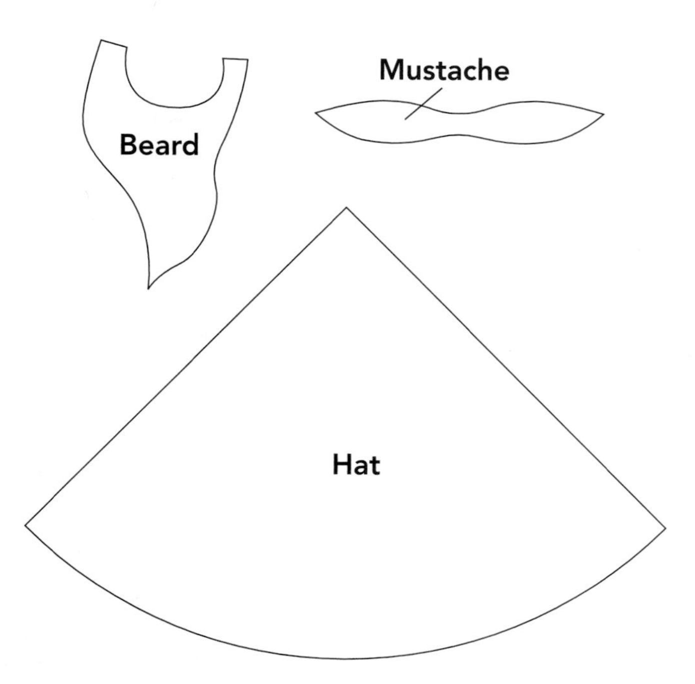

3. Fold metallic thread in half to form loop and knot ends. Curve hat into cone shape, overlapping straight edges and catching knot of hanger in hat tip, and glue. Let dry. Glue hat on cork. Wrap and glue white felt strip around bottom of hat for trim. Let dry.

Directions for snowman

1. Apply 1 coat of primer to cork. Let dry. Paint cork White. Let dry. Dip toothpick into Black and dot on small end of cork for eyes. Paint nose with dimensional paint. Let dry. Draw mouth with marker. Wrap and glue print fabric strip around cork for scarf. Let dry.

2. Cut 1 (1¼"-diameter) circle for hat brim and 1 (1" x 2") piece for hat crown from black paper. Center and poke 1 small hole in brim. Fold metallic thread in half and knot ends. Center and glue knot on small end of cork.

Don't limit yourself to the characters shown here: adapt these directions to make other designs, such as an elf or a bear. For a family or group activity, collect a variety of fabric scraps and trims and let each group member craft a self-portrait cork figure.

Let dry. Thread hanger loop through hole in brim, push brim down to cork, and glue. Roll crown to form tube. Overlap ends and glue. Thread hanger loop through crown. Center and glue crown on brim. Let dry.

Directions for angel

1. Apply 1 coat of primer to cork. Let dry. Paint cork Gold. Paint wooden bead Blush. Let dry. Dip toothpick into Black and dot on bead for eyes. Let dry. Paint eyebrows, using liner brush and Black. Fold metallic thread in half to form loop and knot ends. Center and glue knot on small end of cork. Thread hanger loop through hole in bead, push bead down to cork, and glue. Let dry.

2. Wrap and glue yarn on bead for hair. Cut 1 (3") length of floss. Tie floss in bow. Glue bow to angel at neck. Tie ribbon in bow. Glue bow to back of angel for wings. Let dry.

Botanical Garland

Plastic candy tubes make a delightful garland when filled with red and green foliage.

Materials

- 3 plastic candy tubes with hinged lids (each about 1¼" in diameter and 4" high)
- Gold spray paint
- Florist's foam
- Aleene's Designer Tacky Glue™
- Ice pick
- Assorted red and green foliage and flowers
- Florist's wire
- Tiny pinecones
- Aleene's Satin Sheen Twisted Ribbon™: beige
- 60" length twine
- 24 (4-mm) green wooden beads
- 20 (¾") lengths cut from red plastic cocktail straws

Directions

1. Remove label from each plastic container. Wash and dry each plastic container. Leave container lids open. Spray-paint each container gold. Let dry. Cut 1 (1"-long) piece of florist's foam to fit inside top of each container. Glue foam inside top of container. Let dry. Poke 1 hole through each container from side to side just below rim, using ice pick.

2. For each container, dip stem of each piece of foliage or flower into glue and push into foam to form arrangement. Attach 1 length of florist's wire to each pinecone. Dip free end of each wire into glue and push into foam. Let dry.

3. Cut 1 (17") length of twisted ribbon. Untwist ribbon. Tear ribbon into narrow lengthwise strips. Handling several strips as 1, tie strips in bow. Glue 1 bow to front of each container. Let dry.

4. To assemble garland, knot twine about 18" from 1 end. Beginning with 1 green bead at other end of twine, alternately thread 6 green beads and 5 red straw lengths onto twine. Thread 1 container onto twine. Repeat entire beading sequence with remaining beads, straw lengths, and containers, knotting twine after last green bead.

Duster Santa

Glue felt cutouts onto a lamb's wool duster for an unusual Santa decoration.

Materials
- Felt: red, black, white, peach
- Gold metallic paper scrap
- 8" lamb's wool duster
- Aleene's Tacky Glue™
- Pom-poms: 1 (3/8"-diameter) red, 1 (3/4"-diameter) white
- 2 (6-mm) half-round bead eyes
- Clothespins
- Wooden craft stick

Directions

1. Transfer patterns and cut 1 body, 2 arms, and 1 hat from red felt; 1 belt and 2 gloves from black felt; 1 mustache and 2 cuffs from white felt; 1 face from peach felt; and 1 buckle from gold paper. Lift bottom edge of duster fibers away from handle. Center and glue body to handle. Let dry. With straight edges overlapped, glue 1 glove to each arm. Glue 1 cuff to each arm, covering glove/arm seam. Let dry. Glue belt and arms in place on Santa body. Let dry. Glue buckle to belt. Let dry.

2. Flatten center of duster above body and glue face piece to duster. Let dry. Glue mustache to lower edge of face. Glue red pom-pom nose and bead eyes in place on face. Let dry.

3. Curve hat into cone shape, overlapping straight edges, and glue. Use clothespins to hold edges in place until glue is dry. Glue 1 end of craft stick inside hat along seam. Let dry. Glue free end of craft stick to back of duster to attach hat to Santa. Let dry. Glue white pom-pom to hat tip. Let dry.

If you can't find a lamb's wool duster, substitute a dowel and a large fluffy powder puff. Just glue the puff to one end of the dowel and then complete the project according to the directions.

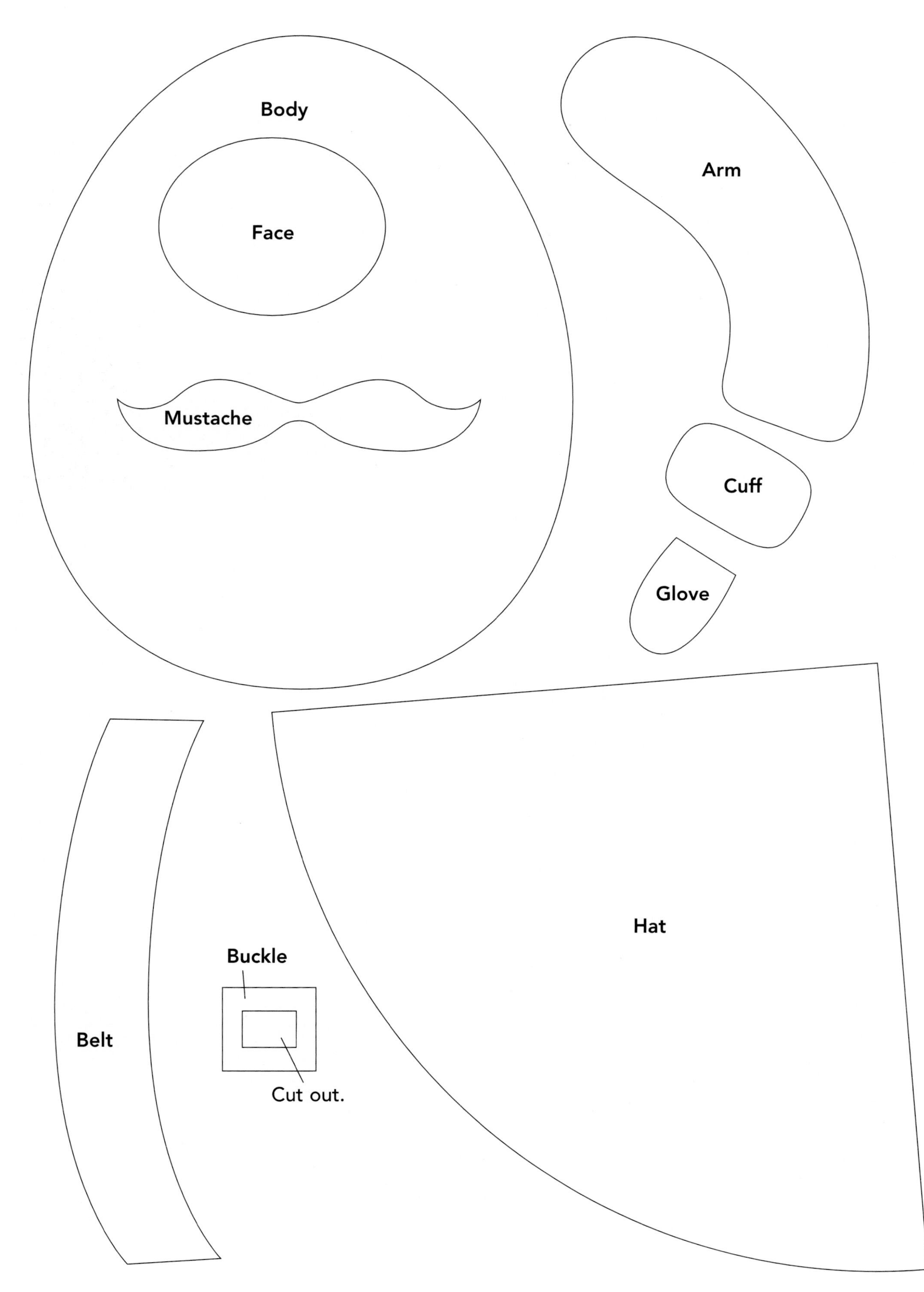
Body
Face
Mustache
Arm
Cuff
Glove
Hat
Buckle
Belt
Cut out.

Stained-glass Globes

Get the look of stained glass with tissue paper and dimensional glue.

Materials

- **For each:** 2 clear plastic dome-style drink lids (each about 4" in diameter and 1¾" high)
- Aleene's Reverse Collage Glue™
- Aleene's Premium Designer Brush™: shader
- Ice pick
- Aleene's Tacky Glue™
- Aleene's 3-D Foiling Glue™
- Aleene's Gold Crafting Foil™
- Beads: 2 (1¼"-diameter) wooden, 2 (4-mm) gold
- Aleene's Premium-Coat™ Acrylic Paint: Gold
- 24" length fishing line
- **For trees ornament:** Aleene's Tissue Paper™: dark green, white, red
- Faceted plastic beads: 4 (6-mm) green, 2 (8-mm) red
- **For multicolored ornament:** Aleene's Tissue Paper™: pink, purple, yellow, light green
- 8-mm faceted plastic beads: 4 clear, 2 pink

Directions for trees ornament

1. Using pattern on page 54 as guide, cut or tear 12 trees from dark green tissue paper. Cut or tear enough small pieces of white tissue paper to cover inside of each drink lid. Brush coat of Reverse Collage Glue inside 1 drink lid. With top of each tree pointing toward top of lid and bottom of each tree about ¾" from rim of lid, press 6 tissue-paper trees into glue, leaving about 1" between each. Brush coat of Reverse Collage Glue on top of tissue paper pieces. Press white tissue paper pieces into glue to completely cover inside of drink lid. Brush coat of Reverse Collage Glue on top of tissue paper pieces. Let dry.

2. Brush coat of Reverse Collage Glue inside remaining lid. With top of each tree pointing toward rim of lid and bottom of each tree about ½" from top of lid, press 6 remaining tissue-paper trees into glue, leaving about ⅜" between each. Complete lid as before.

3. Center and poke 1 hole in top of each lid, using ice pick. Glue lids together around rim, using Tacky Glue. Cut 1 (⅜" x 13") strip of red tissue paper. Glue paper strip around seam of ornament, using Reverse Collage Glue. Brush coat of Reverse Collage Glue on top of paper strip to seal. Let dry.

4. Referring to page 5, make tape tip for bottle of 3-D Foiling Glue. For each tree, draw squiggly outline, trunk, and star with 3-D Foiling Glue. Draw squiggly line on red strip and add dots between trees with 3-D Foiling Glue. Let dry. (Glue will be opaque and sticky when dry. Glue must be thoroughly dry before foil is applied.)

5. To apply gold foil, lay foil dull side down on top of glue lines. Using finger, gently but firmly press foil onto glue, completely covering glue with foil. Peel away foil paper. If any part of glue is not covered, reapply foil as needed.

6. To assemble ornament, paint each wooden bead Gold. Let dry. Thread 1 (4-mm) gold bead on fishing line. Fold fishing line in half. Thread both ends of fishing line through 1 green bead, 1 red bead, 1 green bead, 1 gold wooden bead, hole in bottom of ornament, hole in top of ornament, remaining gold wooden bead, 1 green bead, remaining red bead, remaining green bead, and remaining 4-mm gold bead. Apply Tacky Glue between plastic ornament and each wooden bead to attach each bead to ornament. Let dry. Knot fishing line ends after last bead. For hanger loop, knot fishing line ends about 3" above previous knot.

Directions for multicolored ornament

1. Using patterns as guide, cut or tear the following from tissue paper: 4 pink and 4 purple triangle As and 8 yellow and 8 light green triangle Bs. Brush coat of Reverse Collage Glue inside 1 drink lid. With base of triangle at top of lid, press 1 pink triangle into glue. With base of triangle at rim of lid, press 1 yellow triangle into glue along 1 edge of pink triangle, overlapping triangle edges slightly. In same manner, press 1 light green triangle into glue along edge of yellow triangle. With base of triangle at top of lid, press 1 purple triangle into glue along edge of light green triangle. Glue 1 yellow and then 1 light green triangle to lid as before. Repeat entire sequence to cover remainder of drink lid with tissue paper. Brush coat of Reverse Collage Glue on top of tissue paper pieces. Let dry. Repeat to cover remaining lid with remaining tissue paper pieces.

2. Repeat Step 3 as for trees ornament, using pink tissue paper for strip around seam of ornament.

3. Outline each triangle and draw squiggly lines on pink strip with 3-D Foiling Glue. Let dry. (Glue will be opaque and sticky when dry. Glue must be thoroughly dry before foil is applied.)

4. Refer to Step 5 of trees ornament to apply gold foil to glue. Refer to Step 6 of trees ornament to assemble multicolored ornament, substituting clear beads for green beads and pink beads for red beads.

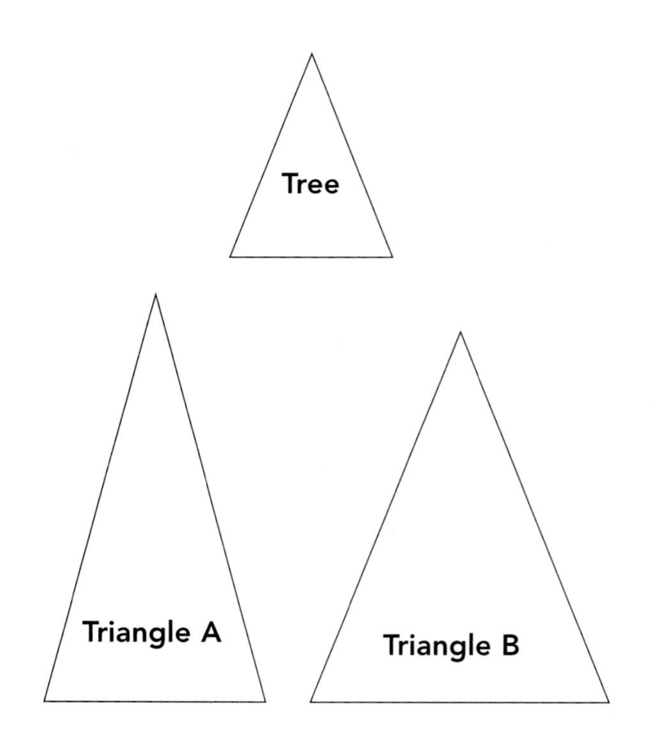

Bottle-Top Ornaments

Save the tops from squeeze bottles of water or sports drinks to make these golden tree trims.

Materials

- **For 1 ornament:** 2 squeeze bottle tops
- Ice pick or drill with 1/8"-diameter bit
- Aleene's Designer Tacky Glue™
- Gold spray paint
- 1 (5½") length 18-gauge florist's wire
- Needlenose pliers
- Assorted beads
- Flat braid or trim scrap
- Gold metallic thread

Directions

1. Wash and dry each bottle top. Center and make 1 hole in each bottle top, using ice pick or drill. With edges aligned, glue bottle tops together around open end. Let dry. Spray-paint ornament gold. Let dry.

2. Curve 1 end of wire into a small loop, using pliers. Thread 2 or 3 beads, ornament, and 2 or 3 more beads onto wire. Curve free end of wire into a small loop, using pliers. Trim any excess wire.

3. Glue flat braid around middle of ornament, covering glued bottle ends. Let dry. For hanger, thread gold metallic thread through wire loop at 1 end of ornament and knot ends.

Decorative Candles

Scented candles take on a holiday glow when embellished with acrylic jewels or plastic mesh.

Materials

- **For each:** Gold spray paint
- Aleene's Designer Tacky Glue™
- Wooden base
- Ribbon (See photo).
- **For metallic mesh candle:** Scented red pillar candle
- Plastic mesh produce bag
- ½"-wide gold-and-black flat trim
- **For jeweled candle:** 1 or 2 plastic paper-holder tubes from adding-machine paper or cash-register paper
- Band saw
- Scented white pillar candle
- Assorted colors flat-back acrylic jewels: ⅜"-diameter, 3/16"-diameter
- Aleene's 3-D Foiling Glue™
- Aleene's Gold Crafting Foil™

Directions for metallic mesh candle

Note: Do not light candle because painted mesh may catch fire.

1. Measure height and circumference of candle. Add 1" to height measurement and ½" to circumference measurement. Cut 1 piece of plastic mesh to these measurements. Spray-paint mesh gold. Let dry.

2. With 1 edge of mesh aligned with top of candle, wrap and glue mesh around candle, overlapping ends. Fold excess mesh to bottom of candle and glue. Wrap and glue trim around top of candle, covering raw edge of mesh. Let dry.

3. Spray-paint wooden base gold. Let dry. Tie ribbon in bow around base.

Directions for jeweled candle

1. Cut plastic paper-holder tubes into ¼"-long sections, using band saw. Spray-paint each section gold. Let dry. Referring to photo, glue ⅜" jewels and gold plastic pieces to candle as desired, using Designer Tacky Glue. Let dry.

2. With 3-D Foiling Glue, apply line around bottom of each gold plastic piece and apply dots to candle between jewels as desired. Let dry. (Glue will be opaque and sticky when dry. Glue must be thoroughly dry before foil is applied.) To apply gold foil, lay foil dull side down on top of glue. Using finger, gently but firmly press foil onto glue, completely covering glue with foil. Peel away foil paper. If any part of glue is not covered, reapply foil as needed.

3. Spray-paint wooden base gold. Let dry. Tie ribbon in bow around base. Glue 3/16" jewels to bow as desired, using Designer Tacky Glue. Let dry.

Santa's Boot Candy Keeper

Fill this container with Christmas treats. You'll never guess what's hiding underneath the festive fabric.

Materials

- 2 half-gallon milk cartons
- Aleene's Tacky Glue™
- Rubber bands
- Stuffing
- 1 (20" x 45") piece of red-and-green print fabric
- Aleene's OK to Wash-It Glue™ or thread
- 16" length 2¾"-wide white pregathered lace trim
- 28" length 2"-wide gold sheer wired-edge ribbon
- 2 red silk flowers
- 4 small stems silk holly leaves with berries
- 6 or 7 cinnamon sticks
- 4 artificial pinecones

Directions

1. Cut off top of each milk carton. Cut 1 milk carton in half. Slip open-ended milk carton half inside other half to reinforce. Referring to Diagram, glue cartons together to form boot, placing open end of half carton next to whole carton. Use rubber bands to hold cartons together until glue is dry. Glue handful of stuffing to end of half carton to round for toe of boot.
2. With right sides facing and raw edges aligned, fold fabric in half lengthwise. Using ½" seam allowance, glue or stitch long edges together to form tube. Let glue dry. Glue or stitch short ends together at 1 end of fabric tube, rounding seam line for toe of boot. Let glue dry. Turn fabric boot right side out.
3. Slip fabric boot onto cardboard boot, gathering fabric on boot to get desired effect (see photo). Turn about 7" at end of fabric to inside of carton and glue. Glue bound edge of lace around inside of carton so that lace extends above top of carton. Let dry.
4. Tie ribbon in bow. Glue bow to front of boot. Referring to photo for inspiration, glue silk flowers, silk holly, cinnamon sticks, and pinecones in place to form arrangement on front of boot. Let dry.

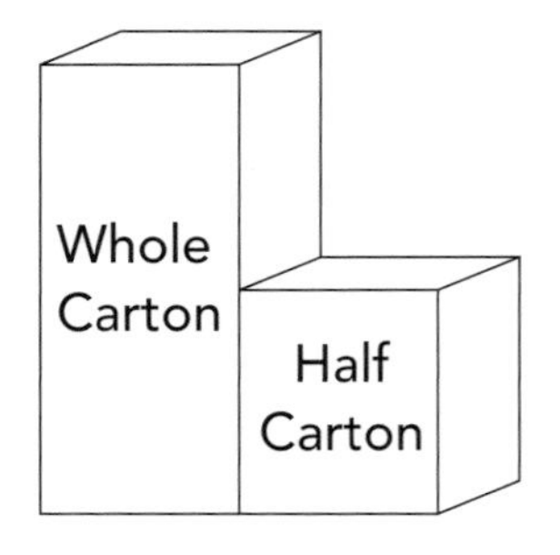

Diagram

Star Tree Topper

Fashion a glittering topper for your tree from brown grocery bag.

Materials

- Brown grocery bag
- 3" square cardboard squeegee
- Aleene's Tacky Glue™
- 22-gauge florist's wire: 24" length, scrap
- Metal comb or kitchen slice guide
- Gold spray paint
- Aleene's 3-D Foiling Glue™
- Aleene's Silver Crafting Foil™
- Tinsel: silver, thin gold
- 50" length ¾"-wide silver-and-gold ribbon

Directions

1. Cut 3 pieces of brown grocery bag ½" larger all around than pattern. With edges aligned, glue 2 bag pieces together, using squeegee to apply Tacky Glue between layers. With edges aligned, 1" of 24"-long wire sandwiched between layers where indicated on pattern, and remainder of wire extending below bottom of star, glue remaining bag piece to 1 side of layered bag, using Tacky Glue. While glue is still wet, transfer pattern to layered bag and cut out star; do not cut through wire. With wire at back of star, squeegee coat of glue on front of star. Rake metal comb through wet glue to imprint lines on front of star. Let dry.

2. Spray-paint both sides of star and wire gold. Let dry. Draw designs on front of star as desired with 3-D Foiling Glue (see photo). Let dry. (Glue will be opaque and sticky when dry. Glue must be thoroughly dry before foil is applied.) To apply silver foil, lay foil dull side down on top of glue lines. Using finger, gently but firmly press foil onto glue, completely covering glue with foil. Peel away foil paper. If any part of glue is not covered, reapply foil as needed.

3. Curve free end of wire into 3 or 4 (2"-diameter) coils to attach topper to tree. Glue tinsel to front of star at bottom. Make multilooped bow with ribbon, securing bow with scrap of wire. Glue bow on top of tinsel.

Star

Cut out.

Place on fold.

Wire placement

Tree Trimmings

Dress up plastic items from your recycle bin to make a pair of jolly ornaments.

Gingerbread Boy

Materials
- 5¼"-diameter white plastic lid
- Aleene's Premium-Coat™ Acrylic Paints: Dusty Beige, Light Fuchsia
- Aleene's Premium Designer Brush™: shader
- Dimensional paints: black, red, silver
- Fine-tip permanent black marker
- Aleene's Tacky Glue™
- Fine glitter
- 16" length ½"-wide red rickrack
- Aleene's Satin Sheen Twisted Ribbon™: green
- 4" length white satin cording

Directions

1. Center and transfer gingerbread boy pattern to top of lid. Paint gingerbread boy Dusty Beige. Let dry. Dip handle of brush into Light Fuchsia and dot on face to paint cheeks. Paint eyes with black dimensional paint. Paint nose with red dimensional paint. Let dry. Draw mouth with marker. Paint details on body with silver dimensional paint. Let dry.

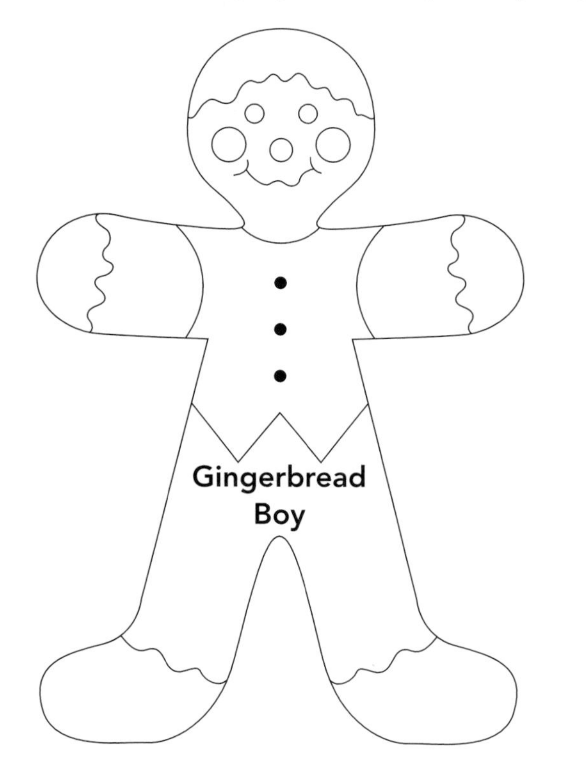

2. Brush thin coat of glue on lid around gingerbread boy. Sprinkle glitter onto wet glue. Let dry. Glue rickrack around edge of lid. Cut 1 (16") length of twisted ribbon. Untwist ribbon. Tear ribbon into narrow lengthwise strips. Handling several strips as 1, tie strips in bow. Glue bow to front of ornament at top. For hanger, fold cording in half to form loop and glue ends to back of ornament at top. Let dry.

Santa's Elf

Materials
- Red plastic candy tube with hinged lid (about 1¼" in diameter and 4" high)
- Craft knife
- 1½"-diameter wooden ball
- Aleene's Premium-Coat™ Acrylic Paints: Blush, Holiday Red, Black
- Aleene's Premium Designer Brush™: shader
- Cotton swab
- Fine-tip permanent black marker
- Aleene's Designer Tacky Glue™
- Felt: blush, green, red
- Pinking shears
- 10 (¼"-diameter) gold jingle bells
- 7" length gold metallic thread
- 6" length ⅜"-wide plaid ribbon

Directions

1. Remove label from plastic container. Cut lid from container, using craft knife. Wash and dry plastic container. Paint wooden ball Blush. Let dry. Dip cotton swab into Holiday Red and dot on wooden ball to paint cheeks. Dip handle of brush into Black and dot on wooden ball to paint eyes. Let dry. Draw eyebrows, nostrils, and mouth with marker. Glue head to open end of container. Let dry.

2. Transfer patterns to felt and cut 2 ears from blush and 2 shoes, 1 collar, and 1 hat from green. Cut 1 (½" x 5½") strip and 1 (½" x 1½") strip from red. Trim 1 long edge of each red strip with pinking shears. Glue 1 bell to tip of each shoe and to each point on collar. Let dry.

3. Glue 1 ear to each side of head. For hanger, fold gold metallic thread in half to form loop and knot ends. Curve hat into cone shape, overlapping straight edges and catching knot of hanger in hat tip, and glue. Glue hat to head. With jagged edge up, glue 5½" red strip around bottom of hat for trim. Let dry. Glue collar around neck, overlapping straight edges at back of elf. Glue shoes to front of container at bottom. With jagged edge down, glue 1½" red strip across top edge of shoes. Let dry.

4. Tie ribbon in bow and glue to elf at neck. Let dry.

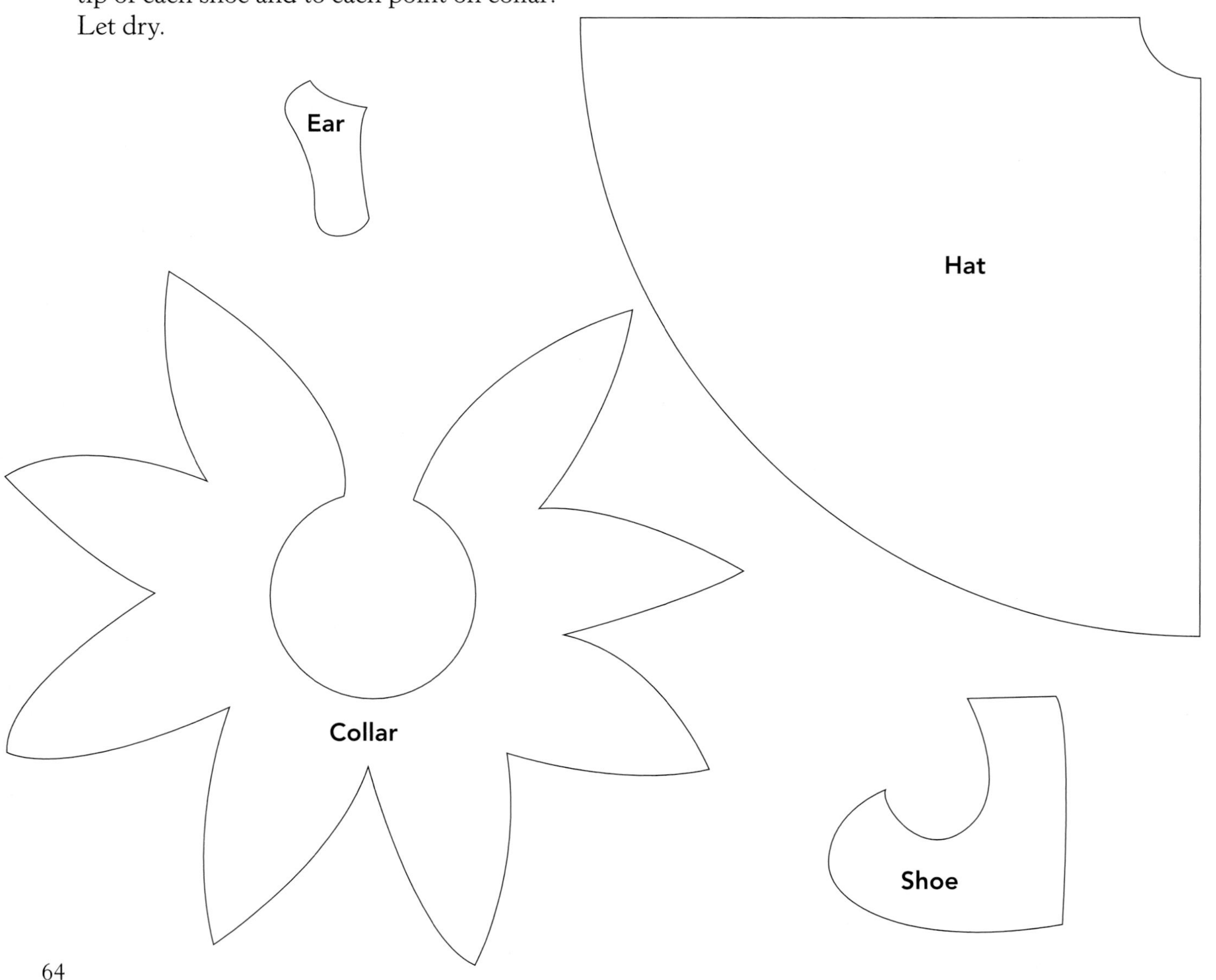

Divine Door Decor

This golden angel, made from window screen, will guard your door throughout the holidays—or anytime of year.

Materials

- Gold metal window screen
- Wire cutters
- 3 wooden craft sticks
- Stapler
- Waxed paper
- Aleene's Tacky Glue™
- Gold metallic chenille stem
- Gold spray paint
- Aleene's Premium-Coat™ Acrylic Paints: Silver, Black
- Aleene's Premium Designer Brushes™: shader, liner
- 3½"-diameter Styrofoam ball
- Serrated knife
- White panty hose or tights scrap
- Pink powder blush
- 20" length 1¼"-wide ribbon
- 18-gauge florist's wire: 2" length, 1" length
- Silver tinsel
- 22" length gold star garland

Directions

1. Referring to Dress and Sleeve Diagrams, cut 1 dress piece and 2 sleeve pieces from window screen, using wire cutters. Cut 1 (12" x 19") piece from window screen for wings, using wire cutters. Referring to Assembly Diagram, curve dress piece into diamond-shaped tube, overlapping points A and B about 2" and inserting 1 wooden craft stick at top of dress for neck. Staple top 2 dress layers together where points A and B overlap. Staple all layers of dress together at neck, catching craft stick in staple. In same manner, shape each sleeve piece.

2. Cover work surface with waxed paper. Apply glue to all cut edges of each piece and glue overlapped areas of each piece together, using liberal amounts of glue. Let dry. Using patterns as guide and referring to photos, draw stars along overlapped area of dress with glue. Draw 1 star at bottom of each sleeve with glue. Let dry.

3. Turn under and crease ¼" along each edge of wings piece. Referring to Wings Diagram, fanfold and gather center of wings piece to measure about 2". Wrap gathered area of wings with metallic chenille stem, twisting chenille stem ends together tightly at top of wings to secure. Squeeze wavy line of glue on front of wings along each short end. Let dry.

4. Spray-paint dress, sleeves, and wings gold. Let dry. Brush Silver paint on each star. Let dry.

5. Cut slice from foam ball to make 3"-diameter flat area for back of head, using serrated knife. Cover front of head with panty hose scrap, stretching fabric taut and gluing edges in place on back of head. Pin fabric edges in place until glue is dry. Apply dots of glue to front of head for eyes. Let dry. Paint eyes and mouth, using liner brush and Black. Dip handle of brush into Black and dot on face for nose. Let dry. Brush blush on face for cheeks.

6. Dip free end of craft stick at neck of dress into glue. Push craft stick into foam ball at bottom of head. Repeat to attach sleeves to angel. Tie ribbon in bow. Attach 2" length of florist's wire to back of bow. Dip wire ends into glue. Push wire ends into foam ball at angel's neck. Let dry. Glue tinsel to head for hair. Let dry.

7. Curve star garland into 7"-diameter circle and twist ends together. Bend twisted ends down at back of halo. Bend 1" length of florist's wire into U shape. Pin straight ends of halo to back of head, using U-shaped wire. To attach wings to angel, bend down ¾" at ends of chenille stem to form right angle. Dip bent ends into glue. Push bent ends of chenille stem into back of head. Glue wings to back of dress. Let dry.

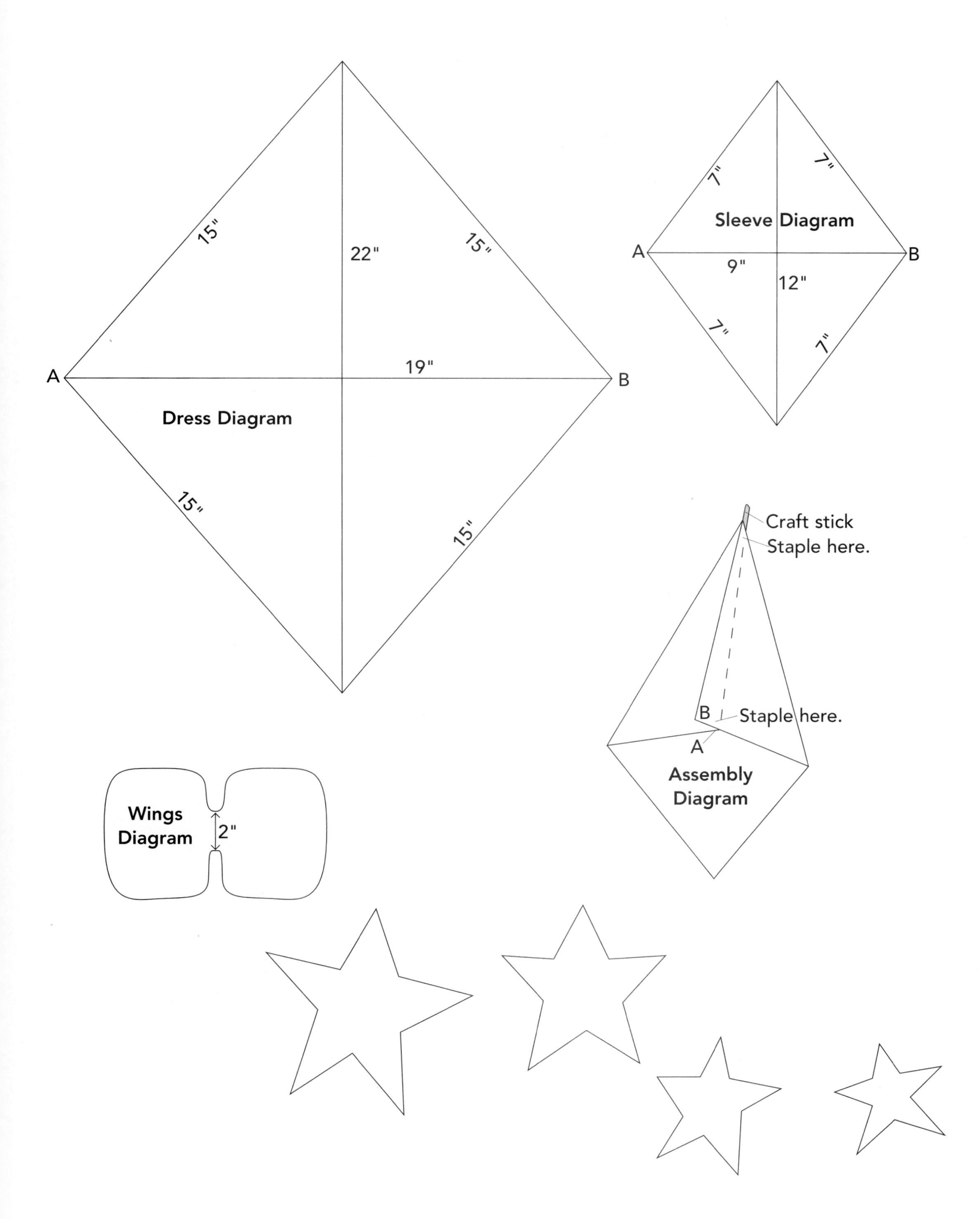
15"
22"
15"
A
19"
B
Dress Diagram
15"
15"
7"
7"
Sleeve Diagram
A
B
9"
12"
7"
7"
Craft stick
Staple here.
B
Staple here.
A
Assembly Diagram
Wings Diagram
2"

Celestial Candle Holders

Collect glass bottles and jars in assorted sizes to make these candle holders.

Materials
- **For each:** Star, moon, and swirl rubber stamps (See note.)
- Gold ink and ink pad (See note.)
- Fun Foam scraps (See note.)
- Foam-core board scraps (See note.)
- Aleene's Designer Tacky Glue™
- 1 or 2 glass votive candle holders, jars, or bottles (See Step 1.)
- 1 metal lid to fit 1 bottle (optional)
- Silver or gold spray paint
- Aleene's Premium-Coat™ Acrylic Paint: Silver
- Aleene's Premium Designer Brush™: shader
- Clear spray polyurethane finish
- 4-mm flat-back clear acrylic jewels
- Silver or gold metallic thread
- Assorted beads

Directions for 1 candle holder

Note: For mail-order source for rubber stamps, gold ink, and ink pad, see listing for Ballard Designs on page 144. If desired, make your own stamps by following these directions: Cut desired shapes from Fun Foam. Cut 1 piece of foam core slightly larger than each foam piece. Center and glue 1 foam piece on each piece of foam core. Let dry.

1. For short holder, glue votive candle holder (right side up) onto shrimp-cocktail jar (upside down). For medium holder, glue top of lid to top of cappuccino drink bottle. For tall holder, assemble medium holder as before. Glue bottom of medium holder to bottom of shrimp-cocktail jar. Let dry. Spray-paint candle holder silver or gold. Let dry.

2. To paint designs on candle holder, ink 1 stamp with gold using ink pad or brush Silver paint on 1 stamp. Position stamp on holder and press firmly, being sure all areas of stamp come in contact with holder. Carefully lift stamp off holder. Let dry. Stamp additional designs on candle holder as desired. To paint dots, dip handle of brush into gold ink or Silver paint and dot on holder. Let dry. Apply 1 or 2 coats of finish to candle holder, letting dry between coats.

3. Glue acrylic jewels to holder as desired. Let dry. Cut several lengths of metallic thread. Wrap and knot thread lengths around neck of holder, leaving long streamers. Thread beads on streamers as desired, knotting thread to secure beads.

Mix and match assorted glass containers to create unusual candle holders. Look for votive candle cups in discount stores to supplement the items you select from your recycle bin.

Welcome Witch

A few items from discount stores or flea markets are all you need to assemble this happy Halloween decoration.

Materials

- Felt: black, white, blush, green
- Yellow yarn dust mop (without handle)
- Aleene's Designer Tacky Glue™
- Small rubber squash
- Plastic coat hanger
- 2 chenille stems
- Black plastic cape or large black plastic garbage bag
- Plastic grocery bags
- Black fabric witch hat
- 1 (1½" x 30") torn strip orange-and-black check fabric
- Plastic spiders: orange, black

Directions

1. Transfer patterns to felt and cut 1 mouth from black and 2 eyes from white. Cut 1 (4½" x 7") oval from blush felt for face, 2 (½" x ¾") pieces from white for teeth, 2 (⅞"-diameter) circles from green for irises, and 2 (⅜"-diameter) circles from black for pupils.

2. Trim excess yarn from center bottom of mop to make room for felt oval face. Glue face to mop. For nose, cut off and set aside round part of squash, leaving remainder of squash about 2½" long. Referring to photo, glue facial features in place. Let dry. Slip hook of hanger inside back of mop. Secure hanger inside mop by twisting 1 chenille stem around hanger hook and mop hardware. Glue edges of mop to hanger as needed. Let dry. Tie cape around hanger or cut opening in garbage bag and wrap around hanger as desired.

3. Stuff witch hat with grocery bags for ballast. Glue witch hat to back of mop. Tie fabric strip in bow. Glue bow to front of witch at bottom of face. Let dry. Glue spiders to cape, hair, and hat as desired. For dangling spider, glue 1 end of floss length to 1 spider. Let dry. Glue free end of floss to hat brim. Let dry. For hanger, poke 2 holes side by side in back of hat just above head. Thread remaining chenille stem through holes and twist ends together, leaving loop for hanger.

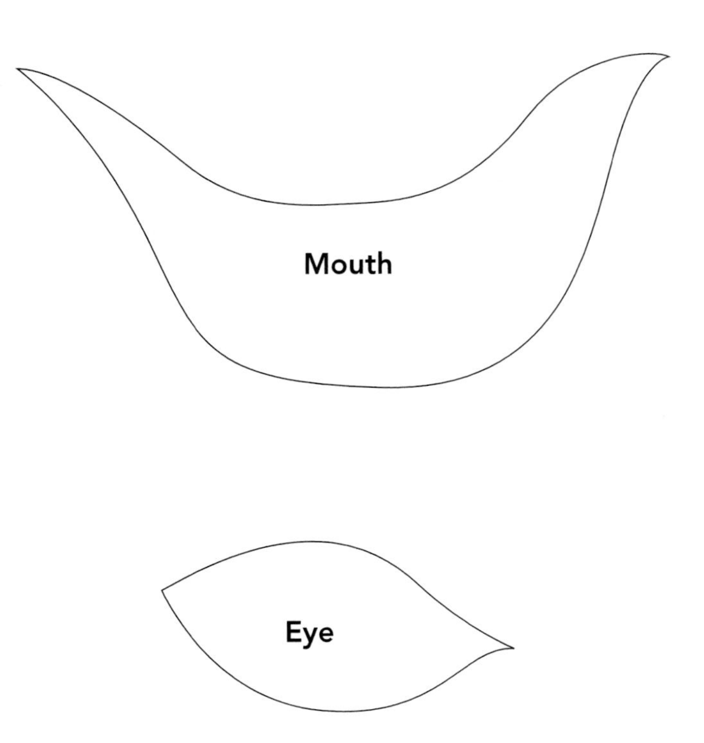

Trick-or-treat Sack

For this fast and fun sack, spatter-paint a pillowcase and draw on spiderwebs. Then add a fat pom-pom spider to each web.

Materials

- Large pillowcase
- Cardboard covered with waxed paper
- Aleene's Premium-Coat™ Acrylic Paints: Black, True Orange
- Aleene's Enhancers™ Textile Medium
- Waxed paper
- Aleene's Premium Designer Brush™: stiff-bristle stencil
- Medium-tip permanent black marker
- Black pom-poms: 2 (2¼"-diameter), 2 (1½"-diameter)
- Aleene's OK to Wash-It Glue™
- 4 (⅜") wiggle eyes
- 8 (7") lengths black satin cording

Directions

1. Wash and dry pillowcase; do not use fabric softener in washer or dryer. Place cardboard covered with waxed paper inside pillowcase. For each color of acrylic paint, mix equal parts textile medium and paint. Cover work surface with waxed paper. Lay pillowcase on waxed paper. Spatter-paint pillowcase, using brush and Black and True Orange. Let dry.

2. For each spiderweb, transfer pattern to pillowcase and draw lines with marker. For each spider, glue 1 (2¼") pom-pom to 1 (1½") pom-pom. Glue 2 wiggle eyes onto smaller pom-pom. Knot each end of each of 4 lengths of cording for legs. Glue spider to pillowcase on top of web, sandwiching legs beneath spider's body. Let dry.

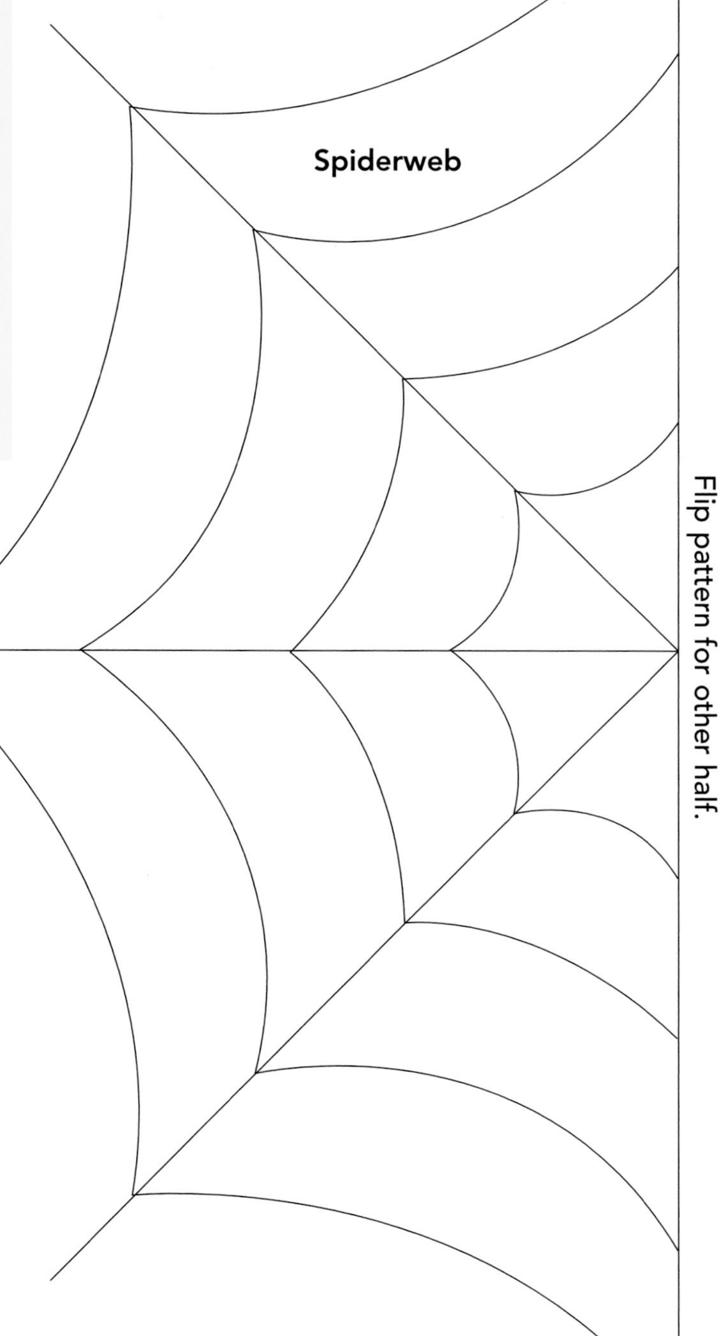

Treat Bowl

Cover a plastic bowl with tissue paper to create a textured surface. Sponge-painted hobgoblins dress up the bowl's rim.

Materials

- Aleene's Tissue Paper™
- Large plastic bowl
- Aleene's Paper Napkin Appliqué Glue™
- Sponge paintbrush
- Black spray paint
- Pop-up craft sponges
- Aleene's Premium-Coat™ Acrylic Paints: White, True Orange, True Lime, Black
- Waxed paper
- Aleene's Premium Designer Brush™: liner
- Clear spray polyurethane finish

Directions

1. Cut or tear large pieces of tissue paper to cover bowl. Crumple tissue paper pieces and then flatten them, leaving some wrinkles. Working over small area at at time, brush coat of glue onto bowl, using sponge brush. Press tissue paper pieces into glue, creating wrinkles to add texture. Let dry. Spray-paint bowl black. Let dry.

2. Transfer pattern to sponge and cut 1 ghost. Cut 1 (1¼"-diameter) circle from remaining sponge for pumpkin. Dip each sponge shape into water to expand and wring out excess water. Pour separate puddles of paint onto waxed paper. Dip ghost sponge into White and blot excess paint on paper towel. Referring to photo, press sponge onto rim of bowl to paint ghosts. Let dry. In same manner, paint pumpkins with True Orange. Paint stem on each pumpkin, using liner brush and True Lime. Paint facial features on each ghost and each pumpkin, using liner brush and Black. To paint dots, dip handle of liner brush into True Lime and press onto rim of bowl. Let dry. Spray bowl with 1 or 2 coats of finish, letting dry between coats.

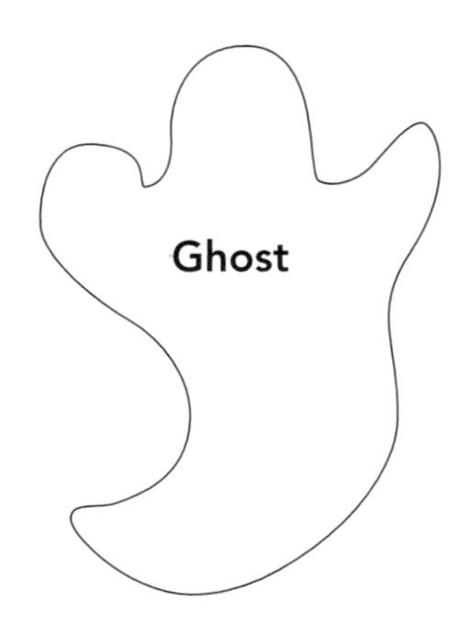

Turkey Table Decor

Liven up your Thanksgiving table with this colorful centerpiece.

Materials

- **For each:** Aleene's Clear Shrink-It™ Plastic
- Aleene's Tissue Paper™: yellow, dark green, red, orange, brown
- Aleene's Reverse Collage Glue™
- Sponge paintbrush
- Waxed paper
- Aleene's 3-D Foiling Glue™
- Aleene's Gold Crafting Foil™
- Aleene's Designer Tacky Glue™
- Gold spray paint
- Red felt scrap
- Aleene's Satin Sheen Twisted Ribbon™: beige
- **For large turkey:** 10"-diameter clear plastic plate
- Quart-sized round plastic jug
- Brown felt scrap
- 2 (3/8"-diameter) plastic eyes
- Black paper
- **For 1 small turkey:** 1 (5/8"-diameter) wooden bead
- 3" length orange chenille stem
- Small pinecone
- 2 (4-mm) black half-round bead eyes

Directions for large turkey

1. Transfer pattern to Shrink-It and cut 2 wings. Referring to wing pattern, cut 4 tissue paper pieces for each wing, using colors as desired. Transfer pattern to tissue paper and cut 22 tail feathers, using colors as desired.

2. Working over small area at a time, brush coat of Reverse Collage Glue on 1 side of 1 plastic wing. Press 1 paper piece into glue. Brush coat of Reverse Collage Glue on top of paper. Repeat to apply remaining paper pieces. Let dry. In same manner, glue tail feather pieces to top of plastic plate (see photo on page 75).

3. For each wing, place wing paper side down on work surface covered with waxed paper. Squeeze line of 3-D Foiling Glue around edge of wing. Let dry. (Glue will be opaque and sticky when dry. Glue must be thoroughly dry before foil is applied.) In same manner, squeeze line of glue on bottom of plate to outline tips of tail feathers.

4. To apply gold foil, lay foil dull side down on top of glue lines. Using finger, gently but firmly press foil onto glue, completely covering glue with foil. Peel away foil paper. If any part of glue is not covered, reapply foil as needed.

5. Use Designer Tacky Glue to assemble turkey. Wash and dry plastic jug. Secure cap on jug. Spray-paint jug gold. Let dry. Transfer patterns to felt and cut 1 large wattle from red and 1 beak from brown. With jug handle at back, glue wattle, beak, and plastic eyes in place at neck of jug. Glue 1 wing to each side of jug. Let dry.

6. Cut 1 (2"-diameter) circle and 1 (1 7/8" x 5 3/4") strip of black paper. Center and cut 1 (1 1/2"-diameter) circle from 2" circle to make hat brim. Slip brim over jug cap. Roll 1 7/8" x 5 3/4" strip to form hat crown. Overlap ends and glue. Slip crown over jug cap. Glue bottom of crown to brim. Let dry.

7. Cut 1 (22") length of twisted ribbon. Untwist ribbon. Tear ribbon into narrow lengthwise strips. Handling several narrow strips as 1, tie strips in bow around neck of jug. To attach tail, glue bottom of plate to back of turkey. Let dry.

Directions for 1 small turkey

1. Transfer pattern to Shrink-It and cut 1 tail. Referring to pattern, cut 7 tissue paper pieces for tail, using colors as desired. Refer to steps 2, 3, and 4 of directions for large turkey to complete tail. Spray-paint wooden bead gold. Let dry.

2. Use Designer Tacky Glue to assemble turkey. Slip bead onto chenille stem so that ¼" at end of stem extends beyond bead. Bend down ¼" at end of stem to form beak of turkey, pressing and gluing stem end onto bead. Shape free end of stem to form neck of turkey. Glue chenille stem neck in place at narrow end of pinecone (see photo). Let dry.

3. Transfer pattern to red felt and cut 1 small wattle. Glue wattle and bead eyes in place on wooden bead head. Cut 1 (6") length of twisted ribbon. Untwist ribbon. Tear ribbon into narrow lengthwise strips. Handling several narrow strips as 1, tie strips in bow around chenille stem neck. To attach tail, slip tail piece between scales at wide end of pinecone and glue in place. Cut 1 (¾") square from remaining Shrink-It. Center and glue Shrink-It square to bottom of turkey for base. Let dry.

Tail

Wing

Broken lines on wing and tail indicate cutting lines for tissue paper pieces.

Tail Feather

Beak

Large Wattle

Small Wattle

Ring of Bunnies

Construct bunny faces from plastic lids and combine them with plastic spoon eggs.

Materials

- 16"-diameter cardboard cake circle
- Fabric: 1 (18") square and 1 (1¼" x 23") torn strip pastel check; 1 (2" x 12") piece each purple print, pink check, yellow check, green check, blue check
- Aleene's Designer Tacky Glue™
- 5 (3½"-diameter) plastic lids
- White spray paint
- Felt: 5 (3"-diameter) circles and 1 (8") square white, black scraps
- 10 (¾"-diameter) pink pom-poms
- 5 pairs ½" wiggle eyes in assorted colors
- 11 heavy-duty plastic spoons in assorted pastel colors
- Wire cutters
- Assorted colors dimensional paint
- Excelsior
- Aleene's Satin Sheen Twisted Ribbon™: white

Directions

1. Center and cut 10"-diameter circle from cardboard circle. Set 10" circle aside for another use. Using cardboard wreath as guide and adding 1" all around, cut 1 wreath from 18" square of pastel check fabric. Center cardboard wreath on wrong side of fabric wreath. Squeeze line of glue around outside edge of cardboard wreath. Fold excess fabric to back of cardboard, clipping curves every 1", and press into glue. Let dry. Repeat to glue inside fabric edge to back of wreath.

2. Spray-paint each lid white. Let dry. Center and glue 1 felt circle on top of each lid. Let dry. Cut 1 (1" x 11") strip from purple print and each check fabric. Ravel edges of each strip. Transfer patterns to remaining purple print and remaining check fabrics and cut 2 ears from each. Transfer patterns to felt and cut 10 ears from white and 5 noses from black. With edges aligned, glue 1 fabric ear to each felt ear. Let dry.

3. To assemble each bunny, glue 2 pink pom-poms side by side on 1 felt-covered lid for cheeks. Glue 1 pair of ears, 1 pair of wiggle eyes, and 1 nose in place on lid. Tie 1 (11") fabric strip in bow. Glue bow to bunny, matching bow fabric to ear fabric. Let dry.

4. Cut handle from each spoon, rounding off edges of bowl, using wire cutters. Set spoon handles aside for another use. Referring to photo, decorate back of each spoon bowl with dimensional paints to look like Easter eggs. Let dry.

5. Glue excelsior, bunnies, and 8 eggs to wreath as desired, leaving space for bow at bottom. Let dry. Cut 1 (32") length of twisted ribbon. Untwist ribbon. Tear ribbon into narrow lengthwise strips. Handling several strips as 1, tie strips in bow. Tie pastel check fabric strip in bow. Glue twisted ribbon bow to wreath at bottom. Glue check fabric bow on top of twisted ribbon bow. Glue 3 remaining eggs to twisted ribbon streamers. Let dry.

6. For hanger, cut 1 (4") length from 1 narrow strip of twisted ribbon. Fold ribbon in half to form loop. Glue ribbon ends to back of wreath at top. Cut small scrap from 1 remaining fabric. Glue scrap on top of ribbon ends for stability. Let dry.

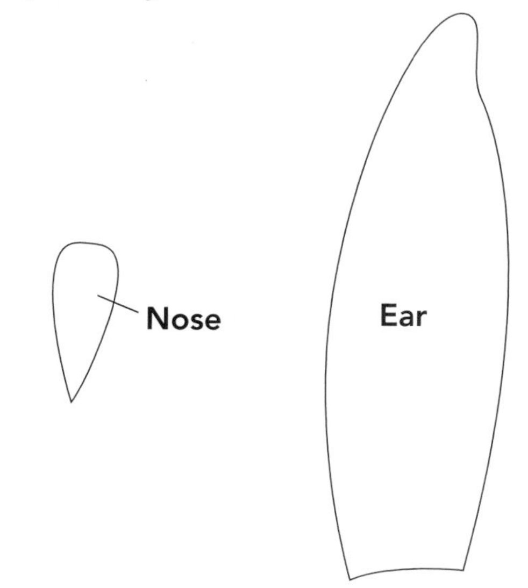

A Pot of Ribbon Roses

A painted clay pot makes an elegant Easter basket when adorned with purchased ribbon flowers and embellished plastic eggs.

Materials

- 5½"-diameter clay pot
- Aleene's Enhancers™ All-Purpose Primer
- Sponge paintbrush
- Aleene's Premium-Coat™ Acrylic Paint: Light Fuchsia
- Wire-edged ribbon: 44" length 1½"-wide variegated pink, 10" length 1½"-wide variegated green, 3 (3") lengths 1"-wide variegated green
- Aleene's Designer Tacky Glue™
- 1"-wide ecru flat lace trim: 1 (19") length, 3 (5") lengths
- 3 (3"-long) plastic eggs
- Assorted ribbon flowers
- Thread

Directions

1. Apply 1 coat of primer to entire surface of clay pot. Let dry. Paint entire pot with 1 or 2 coats of Light Fuchsia, letting dry between coats. Centering pot on center of ribbon, glue pink ribbon to bottom and up opposite sides of pot to form handle. Tie ribbon ends in bow above pot (see photo). Glue 19" lace trim around rim of pot. Let dry. Glue 1 (3") lace length widthwise around each egg. Let dry.

Decorate a painted flowerpot with a profusion of ribbon flowers. Nestle plastic eggs dressed in lace and more ribbon flowers in Easter grass to complete the display.

2. For leaves on pot, cut 10" green ribbon length in half. Referring to Leaf Diagram, fold down 1 end of each green ribbon length to form right angle and then fold left end of ribbon to back along line indicated to form point. Pinch ribbon ends together to shape bottom of leaf. Glue leaves and assorted ribbon flowers onto pot as desired. Let dry.

3. For leaves on each egg, trim each end of each 3" green ribbon to form point. Tightly twist each ribbon at center. Tightly wrap twisted ribbon with thread to secure. Glue leaves and assorted ribbon flowers onto egg as desired. Let dry.

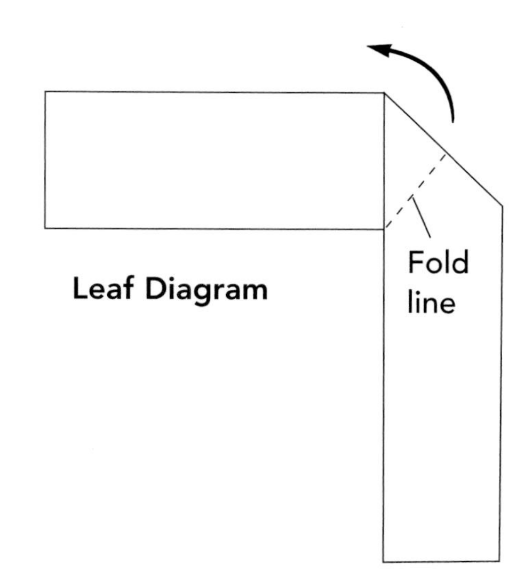

Leaf Diagram

Bunny Basket

Rescue a coffee can from the recycle bin to make this whimsical container.

Materials

- Coffee can
- White spray paint
- Aleene's Premium-Coat™ Acrylic Paints: Light Violet, True Violet, True Yellow, Medium Green, Medium Fuchsia
- Aleene's Premium Designer Brushes™: shader, liner
- 3 cotton swabs
- Drill with 1⁄16" bit
- 1 (22") length 18"-gauge white cloth-covered florist's wire
- Aleene's Satin Sheen Twisted Ribbon™: light blue
- Fun Foam: white, purple, yellow, dark pink, light pink
- Aleene's Designer Tacky Glue™
- 2 (½"-diameter) white pom-poms
- 2 (⅜") wiggle eyes

Directions

1. Wash and dry coffee can. Spray-paint can white. Let dry. Paint can with 1 or 2 coats of Light Violet, letting dry between coats. Paint wavy lines around top and bottom of can, using liner brush and True Violet. Let dry. Dip 1 cotton swab into True Yellow and press on can to paint dots. In same manner, paint additional dots with True Yellow, Medium Green, and Medium Fuchsia, using separate swab for each color. Let dry.

2. Drill 1 hole through each side of can at top. Wrap center of wire around marker to coil. Remove marker. Insert 1 end of wire through each hole in can, shaping wire to fit can. Bend each end of wire up 1" on inside of can. Cut 1 (18") length of twisted ribbon. Untwist ribbon. Tear ribbon into narrow lengthwise strips. Handling several strips as 1, tie strips in bow around coiled wire handle.

3. Transfer patterns on page 84 to foam and cut 1 bunny from white, 1 of each inner ear from purple, 1 tie from yellow, 1 knot from dark pink, and 1 nose from light pink. Referring to photo, glue bunny, inner ears, tie, and knot in place on front of can. Let dry. Glue pom-poms side by side on bunny to form cheeks. Glue foam nose and wiggle eyes on bunny. Let dry. Dip handle of liner brush into Medium Fuchsia and press on tie to paint dots. Let dry.

Easter Egg Gift Bag

Stamp bright eggs across the front of a plain brown bag and then add a yarn bow and a matching gift tag.

Materials

- Fun Foam scraps
- Scissors: scallop-edged, regular, pinking shears
- Paper punches: 1/16"-diameter round, 3/8"-diameter round, 1/4"-diameter round, diamond-shaped, star-shaped
- Aleene's Designer Tacky Glue™
- 1 (2 1/4" x 3") piece foam-core board
- Assorted colors Aleene's Premium-Coat™ Acrylic Paint
- Aleene's Premium Designer Brush™: shader
- Brown paper sack with handles
- Fine-tip permanent markers: dark green, light green
- Brown grocery bag scrap
- Assorted colors acrylic yarn
- Plastic beads in assorted colors and shapes

Directions

1. To make foam stamp, transfer pattern on page 84 to foam scraps and cut out, using scallop-edged and regular scissors where indicated on pattern. Punch holes in cutouts where indicated on pattern. Center and glue foam pieces on foam core, leaving space between pieces as indicated on pattern. Let dry.

2. Paint each area of foam stamp with desired color of paint. Position stamp on sack front and press firmly, being sure all areas of stamp come in contact with sack. Carefully lift stamp off sack. Let dry. Referring to photo, stamp additional designs on sack, applying fresh coat of paint to stamp before each printing. To apply different colors to stamp, wipe stamp with damp paper towel, let dry, and then apply new colors. Draw grass on sack with markers.

3. For gift tag, cut 1 (2 3/4" x 4 3/4") piece from grocery bag scrap, using pinking shears. Fold bag piece in half widthwise to form tag. Stamp 1 egg on front of tag as before. Let dry. Punch 1 hole in tag.

4. Cut several 25" lengths of assorted colors of yarn. Handling all lengths as 1, tie yarn in bow around 1 handle of sack. Thread tag on 1 yarn end, knotting yarn to secure tag. Thread assorted beads on yarn ends as desired, knotting yarn to secure beads.

Bunny Basket patterns

Directions are on page 82.

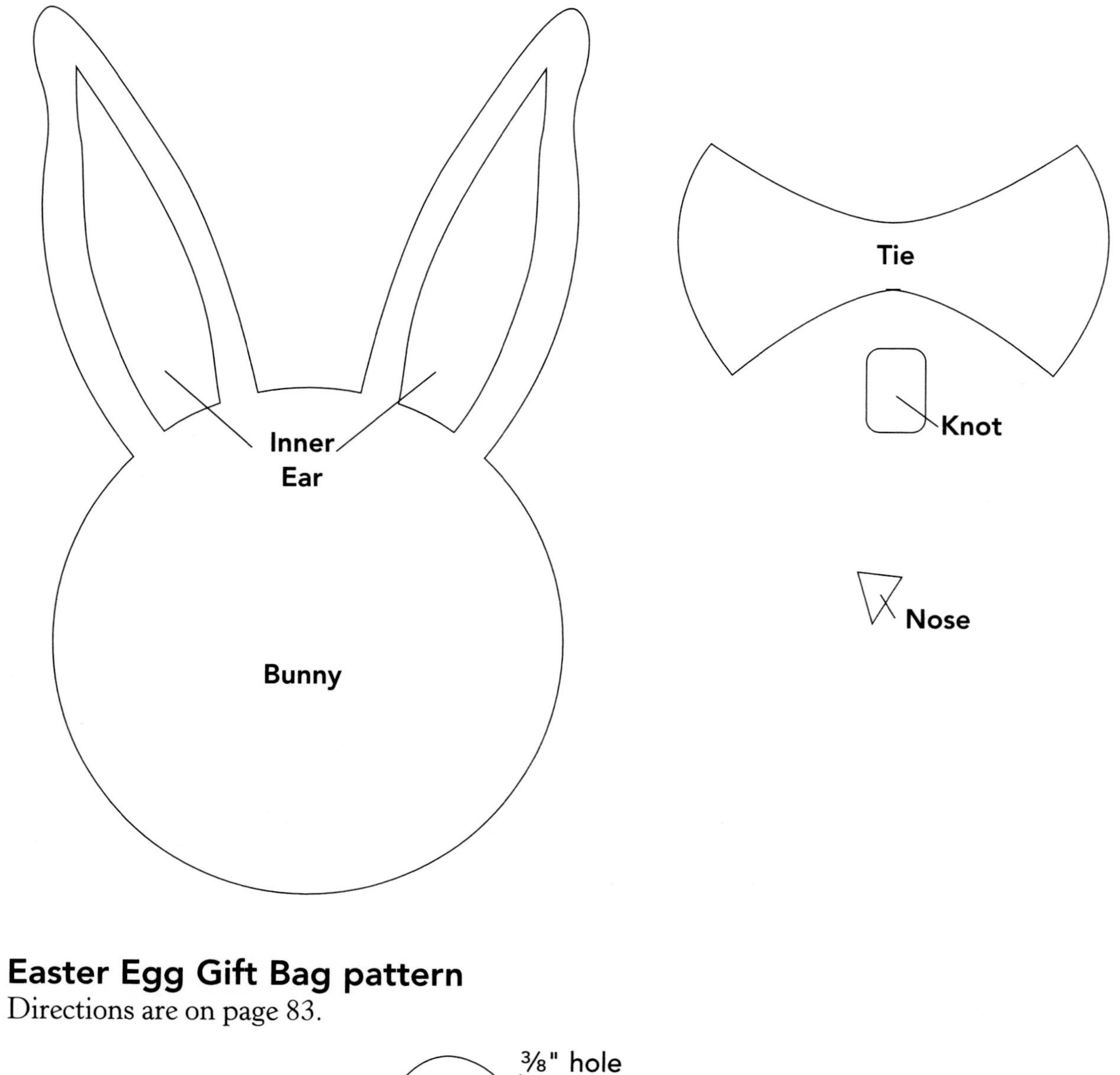

Easter Egg Gift Bag pattern

Directions are on page 83.

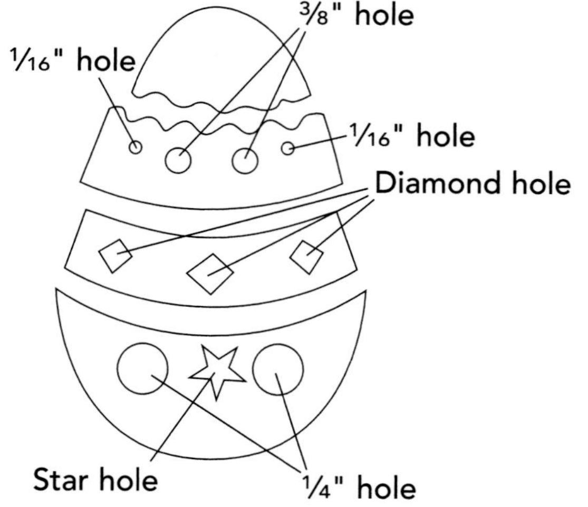

Summertime Picnic Set

Get ready for an Independence Day celebration by decorating a basket, plates, and cloth napkins with paper napkin appliqué watermelons.

Materials

- **For each:** Aleene's Premium Designer Brushes™: shader, liner
- Paper napkins: red, green
- Aleene's Paper Napkin Appliqué Glue™
- Aleene's Premium-Coat™ Acrylic Paint: Black
- **For basket:** Wooden picnic basket
- Aleene's Premium-Coat™ Acrylic Paints: White, Light Green
- ⅞" square sponge piece
- **For each plate and holder:** Clear plastic plate
- Straw plate holder
- **For each napkin:** 14½" square red-and-white gingham fabric

Directions for basket

1. Paint lid of basket White. Let dry. Dip dampened sponge into Light Green paint and blot excess paint on paper towel. Press sponge onto basket lid to paint squares about ⅞" apart around edge of lid. Let dry. Paint basket handles Light Green. Let dry.

2. Transfer patterns to paper napkins and cut 1 watermelon half, 1 watermelon quarter, and desired number of hearts from red and 1 rind A and 1 rind B from green. Cut bite out of watermelon quarter where indicated. Remove bottom plies of napkin to leave cutouts 1-ply thick. Brush coat of glue on basket lid in desired position. Press 1 cutout into glue-covered area, pressing out any air bubbles. Brush coat of glue over cutout. Repeat to glue remaining cutouts and desired number of hearts to basket lid. In same manner, glue hearts around rim of basket and to basket sides as desired. Let dry.

3. Paint seeds on each watermelon, using liner brush and Black. Let dry.

Directions for plate and holder

1. Transfer patterns to paper napkins and cut 1 watermelon half from red and 1 rind A and 11 rectangles from green. Remove bottom plies of napkin to leave cutouts 1-ply thick. Place plate facedown on work surface. Brush coat of glue on bottom of plate. Press watermelon cutout and rind cutout into glue-covered area, pressing out any air bubbles. Brush coat of glue over cutouts. Working over small area at a time, brush coat of glue on top of plate holder in desired position. Press 1 rectangle into glue. Gently brush coat of

Glue tissue paper cutouts onto clear plastic plates and gingham fabric napkins for this picnic set. Decorate straw plate holders with additional tissue-paper pieces to complete each place setting.

glue on top of rectangle. Repeat to glue remaining rectangles around edge of holder, spacing them evenly. Let dry.

2. Working from back of plate, paint seeds on watermelon, using liner brush and Black. Let dry. If desired, omit plate holder and cut 11 or 12 rectangles from green or red napkins and glue them around edge on bottom of plate.

Directions for napkin

1. Wash and dry gingham square; do not use fabric softener in washer or dryer. Ravel edges. Transfer patterns to paper napkins and cut 1 watermelon quarter from red and 1 rind B from green. If desired, cut bite out of watermelon where indicated on pattern. Remove bottom plies of napkin to leave cutouts 1-ply thick. Brush coat of glue on napkin in desired position. Press watermelon cutout and rind cutout into glue-covered area, pressing out any air bubbles. Brush coat of glue over cutouts. Let dry.

2. Paint seeds on watermelon, using liner brush and Black. Let dry. Do not wash napkin for at least 1 week. Wash by hand and hang to dry.

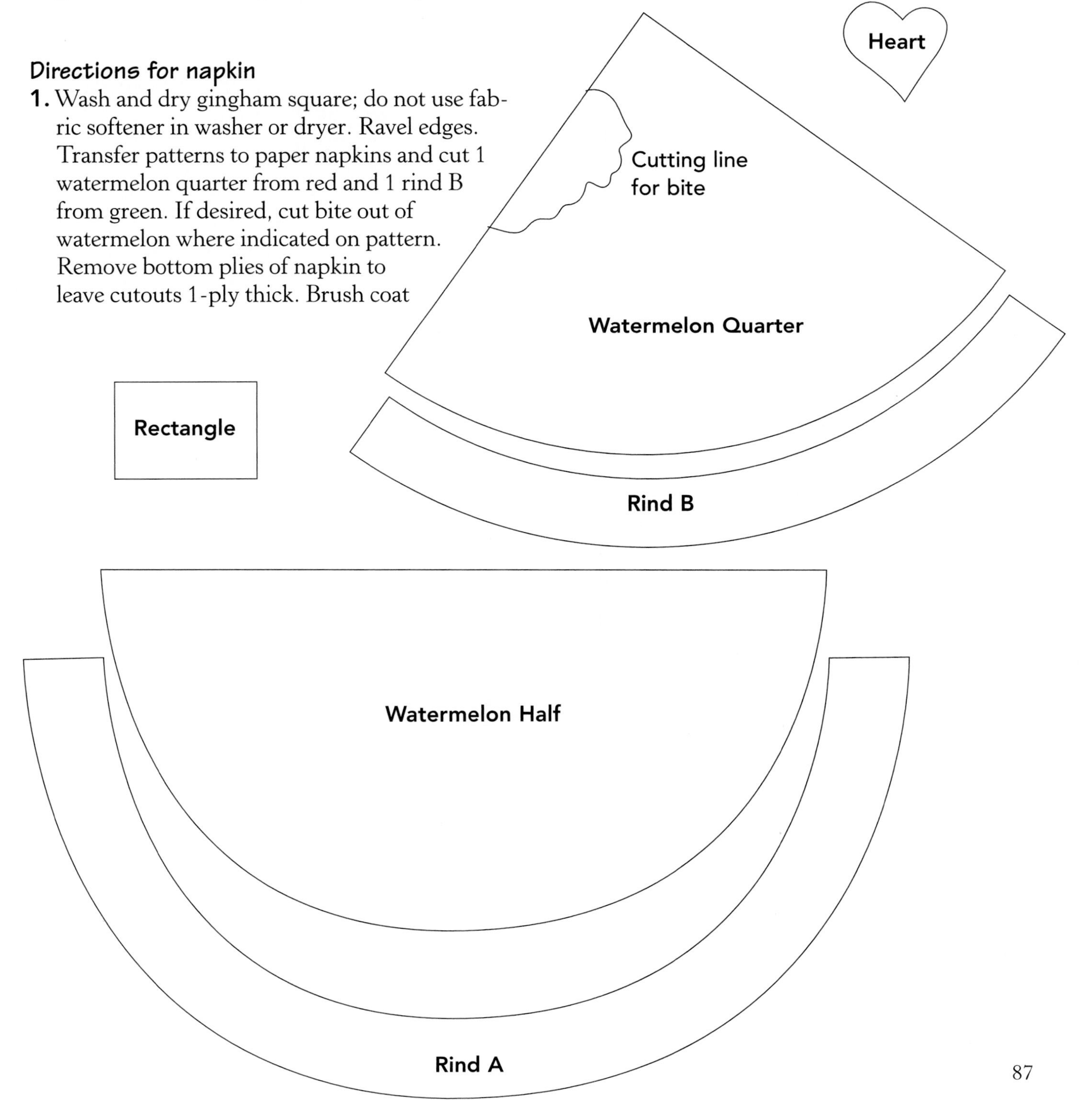

Great Gifts

If you're like me, you get a warm feeling inside when you present someone with a handmade gift. Here are some ideas to get you ready for all sorts of gift-giving occasions. I've also included some quick-and-easy container ideas to make your gifts even more special.

Package Trims

For softly scented decorations, paint car air-freshener leaves and add dimensional details with glue.

Materials

- **For 2 package toppers:** 2 car air-freshener leaves
- Gold spray paint
- Aleene's 3-D Foiling Glue™
- Aleene's Tacky Glue™
- Aleene's Silver Crafting Foil™
- Aleene's Premium-Coat™ Acrylic Paint: Black
- Aleene's Premium Designer Brush™: shader
- Gold paste paint
- 2 (8") lengths gold metallic thread (optional)

Directions for each package topper

1. Spray-paint both sides of 1 leaf gold. Let dry. Referring to Diagram on page 5, make tape tip for bottle of 3-D Foiling Glue. Draw details on each leaf, using 3-D Foiling Glue on gold leaf and Tacky Glue on unpainted leaf. Let dry.

2. For silver-and-gold leaf, 3-D Foiling Glue will be opaque and sticky when dry. Glue must be thoroughly dry before foil is applied. To apply silver foil, lay foil dull side down on top of glue lines. Using finger, gently but firmly press foil onto glue, completely covering glue with foil. Peel away foil paper. If any part of glue is not covered, reapply foil as needed.

For black-and-gold leaf, paint both sides of leaf with Tacky Glue design Black. Let dry. To add gold highlights to glue details, rub finger in gold paste paint, wipe off excess on paper towel, and gently rub finger over right side of leaf. Continue adding gold to right side of leaf until you get desired effect. Let dry.

3. If desired, thread 1 length of gold metallic thread through hole in each leaf and knot ends to make hanger.

Glittery Candlesticks

Painted spice bottles and lids form these sophisticated candle holders. Apply foil to lines of glue for the abstract designs.

Materials

- **For each:** Glass spice bottle (about 1¼" in diameter and 4¾" tall) with lid
- Aleene's Designer Tacky Glue™
- Aleene's Premium-Coat™ Acrylic Paint: Black or Gold
- Aleene's Premium Designer Brush™: shader
- Aleene's 3-D Foiling Glue™
- Aleene's Crafting Foil™: gold or silver

Directions for 1 candlestick

1. Remove label from bottle. Wash and dry bottle and lid. Glue top of lid to top or bottom of bottle, using Designer Tacky Glue. Let dry. Paint candlestick with 1 or 2 coats of Black or Gold, letting dry between coats.

2. Referring to page 5, make tape tip for bottle of 3-D Foiling Glue. Draw designs on candlestick with 3-D Foiling Glue. Let dry. (Glue will be opaque and sticky when dry. Glue must be thoroughly dry before foil is applied.)

3. To apply foil, lay foil dull side down on top of glue lines. Using finger, gently but firmly press foil onto glue, completely covering glue with foil. Peel away foil paper. If any part of glue is not covered, reapply foil as needed.

Textural Frames

Choose from a variety of trash items—berry baskets, packing-foam pieces, and produce bags—and use several techniques to make the frames shown here and on the following pages.

Berry Basket Frame

Materials
- 2 (5" x 7") pieces mat board
- Wire cutters
- Plastic berry basket
- Aleene's Designer Tacky Glue™
- Aleene's Premium-Coat™ Acrylic Paints: Black, Silver, Gold
- Aleene's Premium Designer Brushes™: shader, liner

Directions

1. Center and cut 1 (3" x 4½") rectangle from 1 mat board piece to make frame. Set 3" x 4½" rectangle aside for another use. Referring to photo for design and using wire cutters, cut pieces of berry basket to fit frame. Glue basket pieces in place on frame. Let dry.

2. Paint front of frame Black. Let dry. Paint diamond areas of basket design Silver. Let dry. To add gold highlights, dip finger into Gold, wipe off excess on paper towel, and rub finger over surface of frame. Let dry. Glue remaining 5" x 7" mat board to back of frame, leaving 1 edge open to insert picture. Let dry.

To highlight the geometric design on this frame, paint some sections with silver metallic paint.

Packing-foam pieces create a pebblelike surface on this picture mat. Sponge-paint the foam pieces in colors to match your photo.

Packing-Foam Frame

Materials

- 1 (8" x 10") piece lightweight cardboard
- Aleene's Designer Tacky Glue™
- Packing-foam pieces
- Waxed paper
- Aleene's Premium-Coat™ Acrylic Paints: Black, assorted colors
- Small sponge piece
- 1 (8" x 10") frame

Directions

1. Center and transfer oval pattern on page 95 onto cardboard and cut out to make picture mat. Set oval cutout aside for another use. Spread generous coat of glue on mat. Press packing-foam pieces into glue to cover mat, leaving 1/4" uncovered around outer edge. Place mat between 2 pieces of waxed paper. Place heavy book on top of mat to flatten packing-foam pieces. Let dry. Remove waxed paper.

2. Sponge-paint foam-covered mat Black. Let dry. Rinse sponge thoroughly before dipping into different paint color. Sponge-paint mat with assorted colors of paint as desired. Let dry. Insert mat into frame.

Use a plastic mesh produce bag to cover a cardboard frame.

Mesh Bag Frame

Materials
- 2 (9") squares mat board
- Craft knife
- Aleene's Premium-Coat™ Acrylic Paints: Black, Gold
- Aleene's Premium Designer Brush™: shader
- Plastic mesh produce bag
- Thread
- Aleene's Designer Tacky Glue™
- 1 (16") length black satin cording

Directions

1. Transfer heart pattern at right to mat board and cut 2 hearts, using craft knife. Cut inner heart from 1 mat board heart to make frame. Set small heart cutout aside for another use. Paint frame and large heart Black. Let dry.

2. Cut mesh bag lengthwise into 2¾"-wide strips. Stitch strips together end to end to make 1 (42"-long) strip. Fold 42" strip in half lengthwise and stitch along long edges to make tube. Cut through frame at bottom point of heart. Slip mesh tube onto frame, arranging gathers as desired and overlapping tube ends. Glue mesh in place on back of frame. Paint mesh Black. Let dry.

3. To add gold highlights, dip finger into Gold, wipe off excess on paper towel, and rub finger on mesh bag. Let dry. Tie cording in bow and glue to frame at top. Glue mat board heart to back of frame, leaving top open to insert picture. Let dry.

Packing-Foam Frame pattern

Directions are on page 93.

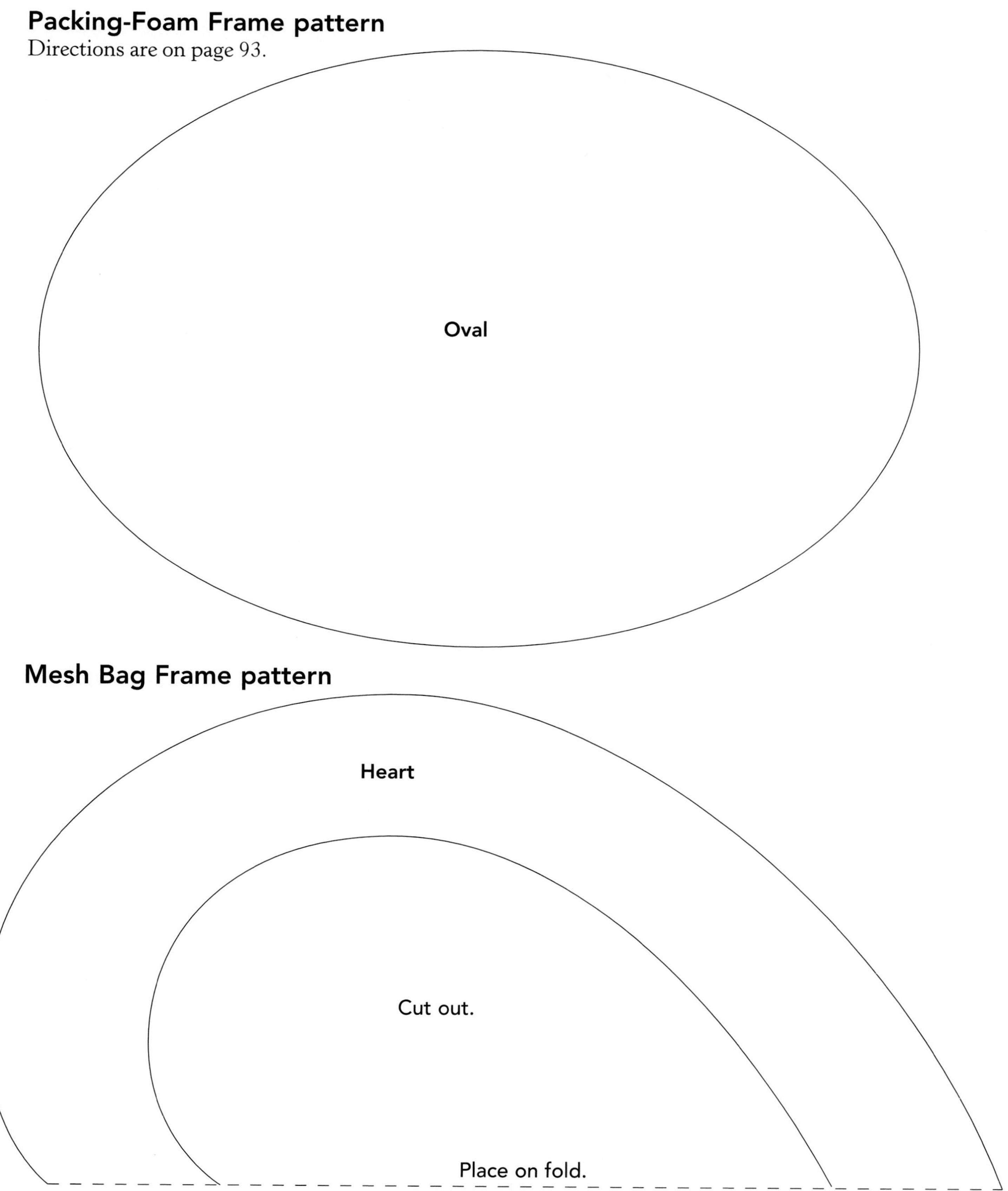

Mesh Bag Frame pattern

Faux Filigree Necklace

No one will ever know you raided your kitchen for the base of this necklace—unless you tell them that it's a piece from a metal steamer basket.

Materials
- Folding metal steamer basket
- Needlenose pliers
- Waxed paper
- Aleene's Tacky Glue™
- Gold spray paint
- 1 piece beach glass or 1 acrylic jewel
- Multicolored novelty yarn (available in knit shops)
- Large-eyed needle
- Assorted beads

Directions
1. For necklace charm base, remove 1 flap from steamer basket, using pliers. Cover work surface with waxed paper. Drizzle lines of glue on convex side of basket flap. Let dry. Spray-paint both sides of basket flap gold. Let dry.

2. Glue beach glass or acrylic jewel to convex side of basket flap. Cut several 10" lengths of yarn. Thread needle with 1 yarn length. Stitch through holes in basket flap to wrap yarn around beach glass or acrylic jewel. In same manner, weave additional yarn lengths through holes in basket flap, allowing yarn ends to hang free. Thread beads on yarn ends as desired, knotting yarn to secure beads.

3. Cut 2 or 3 (30") lengths of yarn. Handling all yarn lengths as 1, fold yarn lengths in half to form loop and knot ends. Thread folded end of loop through hole at top of necklace charm. Thread knotted ends through fold and pull tight to secure.

Fancy multicolored yarn wraps a piece of sea glass on this necklace. Let some of the yarn ends ravel to add even more texture to the design.

Bejeweled Spoon Pendants

In less than an hour you can be wearing one of these dazzling necklaces.

Materials
- **For each:** 1 plastic spoon
- Candle
- Aleene's Premium-Coat™ Acrylic Paint: Black or Gold
- Aleene's Premium Designer Brush™: shader
- Aleene's Designer Tacky Glue™
- Assorted charms, beads, and pearls
- 1 (36") length ribbon or cording

Directions for 1 necklace

1. To bend spoon, hold spoon by bowl end with right side up and place handle of spoon over candle flame. As soon as spoon handle begins to droop, place end of handle directly into flame to melt. Bend handle to back of spoon and press in place, leaving space for ribbon or cording to pass through handle loop. Hold bowl of spoon right side down over candle flame to shape as desired. Remove from heat and let cool.

2. Paint spoon Black or Gold. Let dry. Glue charms, beads, and pearls to bowl of spoon. Let dry. Thread spoon onto ribbon or cording. Tie ribbon or cording ends in bow or knot.

Stellar Coaster Set

Don't throw away those extra computer disks that you get from on-line services. Cover them with fabric to make coasters.

Materials

- **For each:** Aleene's Designer Tacky Glue™
- **For 1 coaster:** 1 (3½") computer disk
- Fabric: 1 (5") square print, 2 (3⅝") squares complementary print or solid
- 15" length desired color piping
- Aleene's Fusible Web™
- **For holder:** Rectangular coffee tin (about 2¼" wide, 4" long, and 2¾" deep) with plastic lid
- 1 (2¼" x 13") strip batting
- 1 (5" x 32") strip print fabric
- Thread
- Gold felt: 1 (2½" x 10½") strip, 1 (3" x 4¾") piece
- 1 (26") length each ⅛"-wide ribbon in 2 colors to match fabric
- Aleene's Opake Shrink-It™ Plastic
- Fine-grade sandpaper
- Gold spray paint
- Fine-tip permanent black marker
- Aleene's Baking Board or nonstick cookie sheet, sprinkled with baby powder

Directions for each coaster

1. Center computer disk on 1 side of 5" square of fabric. Fold and glue excess fabric to disk. Glue piping around edge on wrong side of coaster so that piping extends beyond edge of coaster. Let dry. Center and glue 1 (3⅝") fabric square on back of coaster. Let dry.

2. Fuse web onto wrong side of remaining fabric square. Transfer pattern to fabric and cut 1 star. Center and fuse star onto right side of coaster.

Directions for holder

1. Wash and dry coffee tin. Wrap and glue batting around tin to cover sides. Run gathering thread along each long edge of fabric. Pull to gather and secure thread. With tin centered on width of fabric and arranging gathers as desired, wrap fabric around tin, overlap ends, and glue. Fold and glue excess fabric to inside and bottom of tin. Let dry.

2. Glue 2½" x 10½" felt strip inside tin around sides. Let dry. Trim remaining felt piece to fit outside bottom of tin. Glue felt piece in place on tin. Let dry. Handling both ribbons as 1, wrap ribbons around holder about 1" below top. Tie ribbons in bow at front of holder.

3. Sand 1 side of Shrink-It so that markings will adhere. Be sure to thoroughly sand both vertically and horizontally. Spray-paint sanded side of Shrink-It gold. Let dry. Using black marker, transfer star pattern to painted side of Shrink-It. Cut out star.

4. Preheat toaster oven or conventional oven to 275° to 300°. Place star on baking board and bake in oven. Edges should begin to curl within 25 seconds; if not, increase temperature slightly. If edges begin to curl as soon as star is put in oven, reduce temperature. After about 1 minute, star will lie flat. Remove star from oven. Let cool. Glue star on top of bow on front of holder. Let dry.

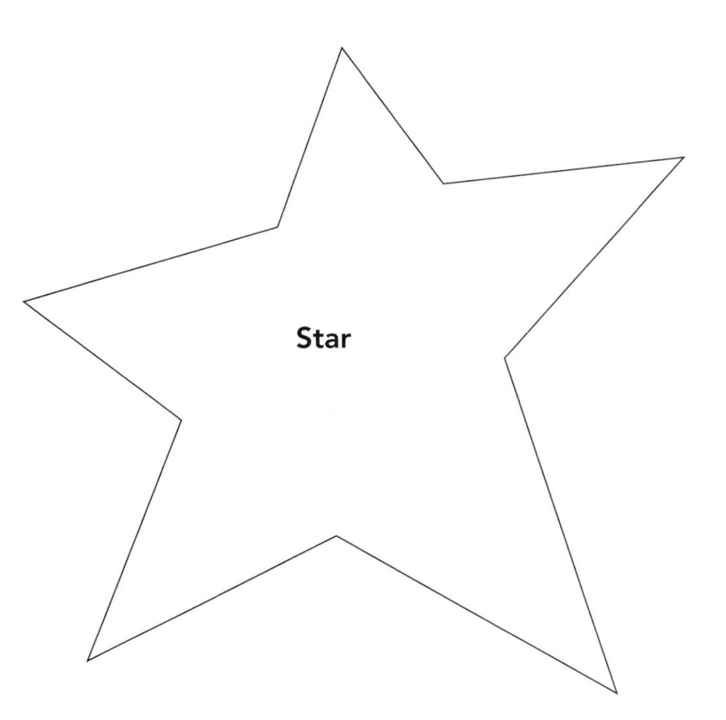

Celestial Shade

Decorate a paper lampshade with print fabric, pop-tops, silver stars, and bead dangles.

Materials

- Lampshade (See note.)
- Gold star print fabric (See Step 1.)
- Aleene's Tacky Glue™
- Spray paints: gold, silver
- 47 pop-tops from aluminum cans
- Aleene's Jewel-It Glue™
- 47 (6-mm) clear flat-back acrylic jewels
- Cardboard egg carton
- Aleene's Fabric Stiffener™
- Aleene's Premium Designer Brush™: shader
- Jewelry findings: 11 head pins, 11 jump rings
- Beads: 22 (3-mm) silver, 22 (6-mm) gold, 11 (½") frosted stars, 22 (5-mm) clear
- Needlenose pliers

Directions

Note: Shade shown in photo is 9" in diameter at bottom. Adjust number of pop-tops, clear jewels, stars, and beaded dangles to fit your chosen shade. If desired, spray-paint a wooden spindle lamp silver to match shade.

1. To make shade pattern, starting at seam, roll shade on large sheet of paper and mark bottom edge of shade as you roll. Realign shade and repeat to mark top edge. Draw line connecting top and bottom lines at each end of shade pattern. Cut out pattern. Transfer shade pattern to fabric and cut out, adding 1" all around. To cover shade, center shade on width of fabric. Starting at shade seam, apply Tacky Glue to shade and gently roll shade on fabric. Continue around shade, smoothing fabric as you go. Overlap ends of fabric, turn top end under ½", and glue. Let dry. Fold top and bottom edges of fabric to inside of shade and glue, clipping curves as needed. Let dry.

2. Spray-paint both sides of each pop-top gold. Let dry. Using Jewel-It Glue, attach pop-tops side by side around bottom edge of shade, centering 1 clear jewel in opening at 1 end of pop-top and extending other end of pop-top beyond edge of shade (see photo). Let dry.

3. Transfer pattern to egg carton and cut 11 stars. Dip each star into water to soften. Brush both sides of each star with fabric stiffener. Let dry. Spray-paint both sides of each star silver. Let dry. Glue 1 star to free end of every fourth pop-top on shade. Let dry.

4. Thread beads on each head pin in following order: 1 silver, 1 gold, 1 silver, 1 frosted star, 1 clear, 1 gold, and 1 clear. Use pliers to form free end of head pin into small loop. Use jump ring to attach 1 beaded dangle to free end of each center pop-top between stars (see photo).

Café
SARKS

All Tied Up

Shop secondhand stores or ask family members for out-of-fashion ties to decorate a lampshade or a journal.

Materials

- **For each:** Aleene's Tacky Glue™
- **For journal:** Leather or vinyl scrapbook with filler paper
- Gold spray paint
- 3 ties
- Decorative cording to assemble scrapbook
- 3 assorted beads or buttons
- Aleene's Jewel-It Glue™
- **For lampshade:** 5 to 7 ties to cover lampshade
- Lampshade (See note.)

Directions for journal

1. Disassemble scrapbook. Spray-paint both sides of each cover gold. Let dry. Referring to photo for positioning, cut each tie down to fit front cover of scrapbook, leaving at least 1" excess at cut end. Glue each tie in place on front cover of scrapbook and turn cut end to inside of cover and glue, using Tacky Glue. Let dry.

2. Reassemble scrapbook, using decorative cording. Glue 1 bead or button to each tie, using Jewel-It Glue. Let dry.

Directions for lampshade

Note: Shade shown in photo is 7" high and 9" in diameter at bottom. Adjust number of ties needed to fit your chosen shade. Heidi cut 15 (10") lengths from 5 different ties to cover shade shown. If desired, spray-paint a wooden spindle lamp to match color scheme of ties.

1. Measuring from each finished end, cut 2 (10") lengths from each tie. Cut remainder of each tie into 10" lengths. Fold and glue cut end to form point at 1 end of each tie section cut from remainder of tie. Let dry.

2. With point extending beyond bottom of shade and side edges overlapping slightly, glue each tie section in place on shade. Turn 1" at cut end of each tie section to inside of shade at top and glue. Let dry.

Thread Scrap Jewelry

If you sew or know someone who does, you'll always have a ready supply of colorful threads for this project.

Materials
- **For each set:** Zip-top plastic bag
- Generous handful of assorted threads in complementary colors
- Aleene's Fabric Stiffener™
- Toothpick
- Aleene's Tacky Glue™
- Assorted beads and jewels
- Pin back
- ⅛"-diameter hole punch
- 2 (8-mm) jump rings
- Needlenose pliers
- 2 fishhook earrings

Directions for 1 set
1. Cut along each side seam of plastic bag to flatten. Lay bag flat on work surface. Place pile of thread on 1 half of flattened bag. Pour small amount of fabric stiffener over thread. Fold other half of bag over thread and press to flatten, saturating thread with stiffener. Open bag and let dry.

2. Peel stiffened thread from bag and cut into desired shapes for 1 pin and 2 earrings. Use toothpick to remove excess stiffener from holes between threads. Glue beads and jewels to each thread shape as desired. Let dry.

3. Glue pin back to back of pin thread shape. Let dry. For each earring, punch 1 hole in earring thread shape. Attach jump ring to hole in shape, using pliers. Attach 1 fishhook earring to jump ring, using pliers.

Handmade Paper

Make your own paper to create a set of note cards or a pretty decorative envelope to fill with preserved flowers and foliage.

Creative Cards

Materials

- **For each:** Handmade paper: 1 (7½" x 11") piece, 1 (5" x 7") piece (See page 107 for directions on making paper.)
- Aleene's Tacky Glue™
- 1 (4¾" x 6¼") piece white paper
- Assorted pressed flowers and leaves
- Toothpicks

Directions for each card

Note: For card at left in photo, Heidi used 1 (7½" x 11") piece of white handmade paper and 1 (5" x 7") piece of handmade paper with flower pieces in it. For card at right in photo, Heidi used 1 (7½" x 11") piece of handmade paper with pencil shavings in it and 1 (5" x 7") piece of purple handmade paper.

1. Fold 7½" x 11" paper piece in half widthwise to form card. Center and glue 5" x 7" paper piece onto card front, using glue sparingly. Center and glue 4¾" x 6¼" paper piece on inside back of card for space to write message, using glue sparingly. (*Note:* It is very difficult to write legibly on handmade paper because of paper's texture. Always glue writing paper inside handmade paper cards.) Let dry.

2. Arrange pressed flowers and leaves on card front to get desired effect. Glue flowers and leaves in place on card, using toothpick to apply small amounts of glue to pieces. Let dry.

To preserve the beauty of summer flowers, press them and glue them onto handmade paper cards. The handmade papers shown at right get their texture and color from common items you probably have around the house.

In the white paper shown under the pen, Heidi used punched circles of colored paper, tiny confetti stars, and glitter. For the purple paper, she added torn bits of purple construction paper to the pulp. Pencil shavings give a woody look to the piece of paper at the bottom of the stack.

Floral Envelope

Materials

- Handmade paper: 2 (6⅛" x 9¼") pieces white with colored paper circles, tiny star confetti, and glitter added to pulp; purple scrap (See at right for directions on making paper.)
- Aleene's Tacky Glue™
- 36" length white satin cording
- Assorted dried flowers and foliage
- Aleene's Satin Sheen Twisted Ribbon™: white
- Silver paint pen

Directions

1. For back of envelope, turn under and glue ¾" along 1 short end of 1 white paper piece to form casing, catching center of cording underneath. For front of envelope, fold down 3¼" along 1 short end of remaining white paper piece. Tear corners from folded end of paper piece to form point (see photo). Glue point down on paper, using glue sparingly. Transfer pattern on page 99 to purple paper and tear out star. Glue star on top of point. Let dry.

2. With edges aligned, glue envelope front to back along side and bottom edges. Let dry. Knot cording ends, leaving 2" loop for hanger. Tie streamers in bow.

3. Arrange and glue flowers and foliage in envelope as desired. Let dry. Cut 1 (26") length of twisted ribbon. Untwist ribbon. Tear ribbon into narrow lengthwise strips. Handling several strips as 1, tie strips in bow. Glue bow to front of envelope at top folded edge. Let dry. Draw star on paper star with silver pen (see photo). Let dry.

Making Handmade Paper

Materials

- 2 (8" x 10") wooden picture frames
- 1 (8½" x 10½") piece window screen
- Heavy-duty stapler
- 1 (5" x 7") piece Aleene's Cotton Linter Paper™
- 1 (6" x 9") piece off-white construction paper or 1 or 2 white paper towels (generic-brand paper towels work best)
- Blender
- ¼ to ½ cup pencil shavings, potpourri, fresh flowers, moss, glitter, bits of thread, punched paper circles, or tiny confetti shapes
- 1 sheet desired color construction paper (optional)
- Plastic dishpan (slightly larger than the mold and deckle)
- Newspaper
- Terry towel
- 1 (9" x 11") piece white felt
- Clean kitchen sponge

Directions

1. Remove glass and backing from each frame and set aside for another use. Stretch screen over 1 frame and staple it in place to make mold. Frame without screen is deckle.

2. Tear cotton linter paper and white construction paper or paper towels into 1" pieces. Put paper pieces into container of blender. (*Note:* If using colored construction paper, tear it into 1" pieces and add to mixture at this point.) Add water to top line of blender. Let stand for several hours or overnight to let paper dissolve. Blend pulp, stopping often to check consistency, until paper is mostly dissolved but not lumpy. (*Note:* If using pencil shavings or other items listed above, add them to blender at this point and blend to mix.)

3. Fill plastic dishpan halfway with lukewarm water. Pour blended pulp into dishpan. Stir to suspend pulp in water. With edges aligned and screen side up, place deckle on top of mold. Dip deckle and mold into dishpan and completely cover screen with even layer of pulp. Slowly lift deckle and mold above water and allow excess water to drain from pulp. Remove deckle and mold from dishpan. Carefully lift deckle off mold and set it aside.

4. To prepare drying surface, stack newspaper (about 1" thick), towel, and felt on flat surface. Turn mold over, with pulp on felt. To remove mold from paper, gently sponge excess water from back of screen. Paper will release from screen when enough moisture has been sponged away. Remove mold and set it aside. Let paper dry overnight. Depending on humidity, paper may take longer to dry. When paper is dry enough to hold together, it can be removed from drying surface and set aside to dry completely.

Cuddly Caps

To make one of these soft baby caps, start with a sleeve from a discarded sweatshirt.

Materials

- **For each:** Sweatshirt sleeve (6" to 8" long from cuff to cut edge)
- Aleene's OK to Wash-It Glue™
- Thread to match sleeve (optional)
- Cardboard covered with waxed paper or Aleene's Opake Shrink-It™ Plastic
- Pop-up craft sponge
- Desired colors Aleene's Premium-Coat™ Acrylic Paint
- Waxed paper
- Aleene's Enchancers™ Textile Medium
- Cotton swab

Directions for 1 cap

1. Turn sleeve piece wrong side out. With right sides facing, glue or stitch cuff opening closed. Let glue dry. Turn cap right side out. Turn cut edge of sleeve up ¾" twice and glue to secure. Let dry. Slip cardboard covered with waxed paper or Shrink-It inside cap.

2. Transfer pattern to pop-up craft sponge and cut 1 heart. Dip sponge into water to expand and wring out excess water. Pour small puddle of desired colors of paint onto waxed paper. Mix equal parts textile medium with each color of paint. Dip sponge into desired color of paint and blot excess paint on paper towel. Press sponge on cap to paint heart. Let dry. Repeat to paint additional hearts on cap as desired. Wash sponge thoroughly before dipping into different paint color. To get shaded effect, dip sponge into 2 shades of same color of paint and blot excess paint on paper towel. To paint dots around edge of each heart, dip cotton swab into desired color of paint and dot on cap. Let dry.

Use your imagination to create a whole wardrobe of baby caps. Other patterns in this book that would work well for these caps are the flowers on page 30 and the angels on page 125.

For a Christmas cap, use a photocopier to reduce the gingerbread boy pattern on page 63 and then paint it on the cap. With the stamp from the Gift Bag on page 83, you'll have a Easter bonnet for a baby in no time.

Changing-Table Caddy

Create a handy organizer for Baby's room from fabric-covered plastic containers.

Materials

- Plastic containers: 1 (2½" wide, 5½" long, and 6¼" deep), 1 (2¼" wide, 4" long, and 3" deep), 1 (2" wide, 4" long, and 2" deep)
- Batting: 1 (6" x 16") piece, 1 (3" x 12¼") piece, 1 (2" x 12¼") piece
- Aleene's Tacky Glue™
- Pastel print fabric: 1 (11" x 16¼") piece, 1 (7" x 12½") piece, (5" x 12½") piece
- Rickrack in assorted colors and widths: 1 (16") length, 2 (12¼") lengths
- ⅛"-wide satin ribbon: 48" length light purple, 32" length light blue, 32" length light yellow
- Florist's wire scraps
- 3 large white ribbon roses

Directions

Note: If you can't find containers like ones Heidi used, be sure to adjust amount of batting, fabric, and rickrack needed to fit your containers.

1. Wash and dry each plastic container. Wrap and glue 1 batting piece to cover each corresponding container. With container centered on width of fabric, wrap and glue 1 fabric piece around each corresponding container, overlapping ends. Fold and glue excess fabric to bottom and inside of container. Let dry.

2. Wrap and glue 1 length of rickrack around each corresponding container, placing rickrack about ½" from top of container. Let dry.

3. Cut 1 (18") length from each color of ribbon. Handling all lengths as 1, make multilooped bow with 18" ribbon lengths. Secure bow with 1 scrap of florist's wire. Referring to photo, glue bow to front of large container. Glue 1 ribbon rose on top of bow. Let dry. Cut remaining light purple ribbon in half. Handling both ribbons as 1, make multilooped bow with 1 light purple length and remaining yellow length. Secure bow with 1 scrap of florist's wire. In same manner, make another multilooped bow with remaining ribbon lengths. Referring to photo, glue 1 bow to each remaining container. Glue 1 ribbon rose on top of each bow. Let dry.

4. Referring to photo, glue containers together to form caddy. Let dry.

Treasure Box

Use purchased stencils to cut the letters of your child's name or a favorite saying and fuse them onto this box.

Materials

- 87-ounce laundry detergent box
- Craft knife
- Fabric: 1 (10" x 28½") piece and 1 (10" x 13½") piece print, solid to match print
- Aleene's Tacky Glue™
- Medium-weight cardboard (optional)
- Black spray paint
- Aleene's Fusible Web™
- 2"-high block-style alphabet stencils

Directions

1. If needed, cut lid from box, using craft knife. Trim excess cardboard to make all sides of lid same size. If needed, remove cardboard insert from box. Turn under and glue ½" along 1 long edge of 10" x 28½" print fabric. With 1½" of fabric extending beyond top edge of box, wrap and glue fabric around box to cover sides, overlapping 28½" edges with hemmed edge on top. Fold and glue excess fabric to inside and bottom of box. Let dry.

2. Center top of lid on wrong side of remaining print fabric. Fold and glue excess fabric to inside of lid. Let dry.

3. If needed, make cardboard insert for box as follows: Measure depth and circumference of box. Add 1" to each measurement and cut cardboard to these measurements. Beginning 2" from 1 end of cardboard, mark and score lines across width of cardboard to match width of each side of box. Fold cardboard along scored lines, overlap ends, and glue. Let dry. Spray-paint cardboard insert black. Let dry. Slip cardboard inside box.

4. Fuse web onto wrong side of solid fabric. Reverse desired letters and transfer to solid fabric. Cut out letters. Fuse letters onto front of box. Put lid on box.

Cow Bank

Add dowel legs and a foam egg head to a plastic bottle to make this bovine bank.

Materials

- Quart-sized rectangular plastic bottle
- 3"-long Styrofoam egg
- Knives: serrated, craft
- Aleene's Designer Tacky Glue™
- 4 (2¼") lengths ⅝"-diameter wooden dowel
- Aleene's Tissue Paper™: white
- Aleene's Paper Napkin Appliqué Glue™
- Aleene's Premium Designer Brush™: shader
- Aleene's Premium-Coat™ Acrylic Paints: White, Black
- Felt scraps: black, pink
- 3⁄16"-diameter hole punch
- 2 (⅜"-long) black-and-white plastic eyes
- Fine-tip permanent black marker
- Aleene's Satin Sheen Twisted Ribbon™: white scrap
- Small cow bell
- 16" length ¼"-wide blue satin ribbon

Directions

1. Wash and dry plastic bottle. Referring to photo for orientation, press egg onto bottle neck to form indentation. Using serrated knife, carve hole in egg for neck of bottle. Apply Designer Tacky Glue to neck of bottle and press egg onto bottle neck. Centering slit on cow's back, cut 1 (⅛" x 1½") slit in narrow side of bottle for money slot (see photo). Using dowel as guide, cut 2 holes side by side on bottom of cow, about ¾" from each end, to insert dowel legs. Glue 1 dowel in each hole in bottle, pushing ½" at end of dowel into hole and using Designer Tacky Glue. Let dry.

2. Cut pieces of tissue paper to cover bottle and egg. Brush coat of Napkin Appliqué Glue on bottle and egg. Press tissue paper pieces into glue-covered area to cover entire surface of bottle and egg. Brush coat of Napkin Appliqué Glue on top of tissue paper. Let dry. Cut opening in tissue paper to match money slot. Paint entire cow White. Let dry. Paint hoof at bottom of each leg and spots on cow Black (see photo). Let dry.

3. Transfer pattern to black felt and cut 2 ears. Punch 2 circles from pink felt for nostrils. Glue ears, nostrils, and plastic eyes on cow, using Designer Tacky Glue. Let dry. Draw mouth on cow with marker. Cut 1 (¼" x 5") strip from twisted ribbon scrap. Trim 1 end of strip to form point. Glue other end of strip to cow for tail, using Designer Tacky Glue. Let dry. Thread bell onto ribbon. Tie ribbon in bow around cow's neck.

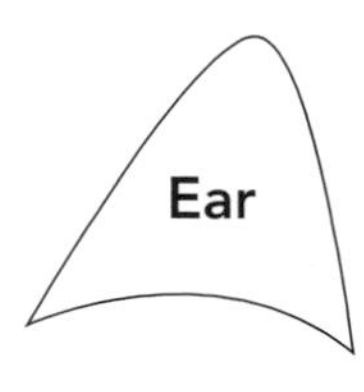

Let your child do the gluing and the painting on this cow-bank project. Consider using a foam ball instead of an egg and changing the paint colors to create another kind of animal.

Trinket Boxes

Combine floral gift wrap with dried flowers and foliage to transform a small container into a pretty dresser accessory or a small gift box.

Materials

- **For each:** Rectangular coffee tin (about 2¼" wide, 4" long, and 2¾" deep) with plastic lid
- Gold spray paint
- Floral gift wrap
- Aleene's Instant Decoupage Glue™
- Sponge paintbrush
- Moss
- Assorted silk or dried flowers and foliage
- Aleene's Designer Tacky Glue™

Directions for 1 box

1. Wash and dry coffee tin and lid. Spray-paint tin and lid gold. Let dry. Cut 2 (2½" x 6¼") strips of gift wrap. Brush coat of Instant Decoupage Glue on 1 side and 1 end of tin. Brush coat of Instant Decoupage Glue on wrong side of 1 strip of paper. With long edge of paper aligned with bottom edge of lip of tin, press paper onto glued area of tin. Brush coat of Instant Decoupage Glue on top of paper, pressing out any air bubbles. In same manner, glue remaining paper strip to other side and other end of tin, slightly overlapping ends of previous paper strip. Let dry. Brush another coat of Instant Decoupage Glue on top of paper. Let dry. Trim any excess paper at bottom of tin.

2. Glue moss, flowers, and foliage to lid, using Designer Tacky Glue. Let dry.

Gift Pot

Spatter-paint a clay flowerpot and saucer to create this charming gift container.

Materials
- Aleene's Enhancers™ All-Purpose Primer
- Sponge paintbrush
- Clay pot (about 6⅜" in diameter and 5" high)
- Clay saucer (about 6⅞" in diameter at top, to fit over open end of pot)
- Aleene's Premium-Coat™ Acrylic Paints: True Yellow, True Apricot, True Orange, Deep Fuchsia, Deep Violet
- Aleene's Premium Designer Brush™: stiff-bristle stencil
- Aleene's Satin Sheen Twisted Ribbon™: yellow, pink, blue, light green, beige, white
- Aleene's Designer Tacky Glue™

Directions

1. Apply 1 coat of primer to outside of pot and bottom of saucer, using sponge brush. Let dry. Working with 1 paint color at a time, spatter-paint outside of pot and bottom of saucer with paints as desired, using stiff-bristle stencil brush. Let dry.

2. Cut 1 (42") length from each color of twisted ribbon. Untwist each ribbon. Tear each ribbon into narrow lengthwise strips. Handling several strips of each color as 1, tie strips in bow. Place gift inside pot. With painted side up, place saucer on top of pot for lid. Center and glue bow on lid. Let dry. To keep saucer from slipping off pot, knot several streamer ends from opposite sides of bow at bottom of pot. Trim remaining streamers as desired.

Star-studded Canister

Silver paint makes a cardboard food canister gleam. Add dimensional gold stars for a stellar gift presentation.

Materials

- Cardboard food canister (about 5⅛" in diameter and 7" high) with plastic lid
- Silver spray paint
- Pop-up craft sponge
- Waxed paper
- Aleene's 3-D Foiling Glue™
- Aleene's Gold Crafting Foil™
- 34" length 2"-wide gold mesh wire-edged ribbon
- Florist's wire scrap
- 2 (14") lengths gold metallic star garland
- Fine gold tinsel

Directions

1. Wash and dry canister and lid. Spray-paint canister and lid silver. Let dry. Transfer pattern to pop-up craft sponge and cut 1 star. Dip sponge into water and wring out excess water.

2. Pour small puddle of glue onto waxed paper. Dip sponge into glue and press onto canister in desired position. Repeat to apply additional glue stars to canister. Let dry. (Glue will be opaque and sticky when dry. Glue must be thoroughly dry before foil is applied.)

3. To apply gold foil, lay foil dull side down on top of glue stars. Using finger, gently but firmly press foil onto glue, completely covering glue with foil. Peel away foil paper. If any part of glue is not covered, reapply foil as needed.

4. Make multilooped bow with gold ribbon. Secure bow with florist's wire. Working from top of lid, center and poke wire ends through plastic lid. Bend wire ends down to secure bow. Wrap each length of star garland around marker to coil. Remove marker. To attach garland to lid, bend center of each coiled garland length around bottom of bow. Place gift inside canister. Snap lid on canister, catching small handful of tinsel beneath edge of lid.

Quick Gift Sacks

Jazz up a plain brown wrapper with a motif cut from a paper napkin.

Materials

- **For each:** Print paper napkin
- Aleene's Paper Napkin Appliqué Glue™
- Sponge paintbrush
- Brown paper sack
- Satin ribbon or raffia to match napkin
- Aleene's Tacky Glue™
- Fine-tip permanent markers to match napkin (optional)

Directions for 1 sack

1. Cut desired motif from paper napkin. Remove bottom plies of napkin to leave cutout 1-ply thick. Brush very thin coat of Napkin Appliqué Glue on sack in desired position. Press cutout into glue-covered area, pressing out any air bubbles. Brush thin coat of Napkin Appliqué Glue on top of cutout. Let dry.

2. Tie ribbon in bow. Glue bow to sack, using Tacky Glue. If desired, embellish front of sack with markers.

Treasure Trove

This chapter is brimming with attractive and useful designs for you to make just for yourself. Choose from projects like a lace-covered dresser set, the colander wind chimes, or a set of kitchen canisters—and let your creativity shine.

Gilded Leaves Table Linens

Stencil metallic leaves on a purchased mat and napkin. Then add an easy matching napkin ring.

Materials

- **For each set:** Purchased ivory fabric mat and napkin
- Plastic lid at least 3½" in diameter (See Step 1.)
- Craft knife
- Aleene's Premium-Coat™ Acrylic Paints: Gold, Silver, Copper
- Aleene's Enhancers™ Textile Medium
- Aleene's Premium Designer Brushes™: stiff-bristle stencil, liner
- Pencil with eraser
- Gold spray paint
- 1 (½" x 5½") strip cardboard
- Aleene's Designer Tacky Glue™
- Clothespin
- Aleene's Satin Sheen Twisted Ribbon™: beige

Directions for 1 set

1. **For mat and napkin,** wash and dry mat and napkin; do not use fabric softener in washer or dryer. Wash and dry plastic lid. Center and transfer pattern on plastic lid and cut out leaf to make stencil. Set leaf cutout aside for use in Step 3. For each color of acrylic paint, mix equal parts textile medium and paint.

2. Place leaf stencil on mat in desired position. Stencil leaf on mat with Gold. Carefully remove stencil from mat. Let dry. Repeat to stencil additional leaves on mat and napkin (see photo). Paint vines and vein on each leaf, using liner brush and Silver. Let dry. Dip pencil eraser into Copper and press onto mat and napkin to paint berries as desired. Let dry.

3. **For napkin ring,** spray-paint both sides of leaf cutout gold. Let dry. Paint vein on 1 side of leaf, using liner brush and Silver. Let dry. Curve cardboard strip into ring, overlap ends ¼", and glue. Use clothespin to hold ends in place until glue is dry. Cut 1 (26") length of twisted ribbon. Tear ribbon into ½"-wide strips. Wrap and glue cardboard ring with ½"-wide ribbon strips to cover. Let dry.

4. Trim 1 remaining strip to 10" in length. Tear 10" length into narrow lengthwise strips. Handling several narrow strips as 1, tie strips in bow. Glue leaf onto ring. Glue bow on top of leaf. Let dry.

To stencil table linens, transfer the pattern given here to a plastic lid from a tub of butter or a can of coffee. Save the leaf cutout, paint it, and then glue it onto the napkin ring. You'll need one plastic lid for each place setting you make.

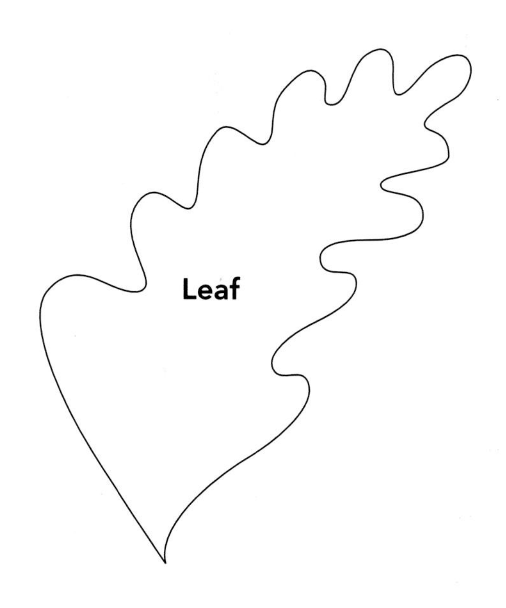

Denim Place Setting

Glue a napkin-holding pocket from a pair of worn-out blue jeans onto a denim mat. Add sponge-painted details for a finishing touch.

Materials

- **For each set:** Back pocket from blue jeans
- Purchased denim place mat and napkin (See note.)
- Aleene's OK to Wash-It Glue™
- Pop-up craft sponge
- Aleene's Premium-Coat™ Acrylic Paints: Deep Blue, White, Silver
- Waxed paper
- Aleene's Enhancers™ Textile Medium
- Pencil with eraser

Directions for 1 set

Note: If you prefer, cut 1 (12¾" x 17½") piece and 1 (17¼") square from lightweight denim fabric. Trim corners from 12¾" x 17" piece for place mat (see photo). Turn under ¼" along edges of each denim piece and hem. Complete place setting as described below.

1. Wash and dry pocket, mat, and napkin; do not use fabric softener in washer or dryer. Squeeze line of glue around side and bottom edges on wrong side of pocket. Referring to photo for positioning, glue pocket in place on left end of mat. Let dry. Transfer pattern to pop-up craft sponge and cut 1 diamond. Dip sponge into water to expand and wring out excess water.

2. Pour separate puddles of paint onto waxed paper. Mix equal parts textile medium with each color of paint. Dip sponge into Deep Blue and blot excess paint on paper towel. Referring to photo, press sponge onto pocket. Repeat to paint 2 more diamonds on pocket. Let dry. Rinse sponge thoroughly before dipping into different paint color. Dip pencil eraser into White and press onto pocket to paint dots between diamonds. Let dry. In same manner, paint white diamonds and silver dots around edge of mat and napkin. Let dry.

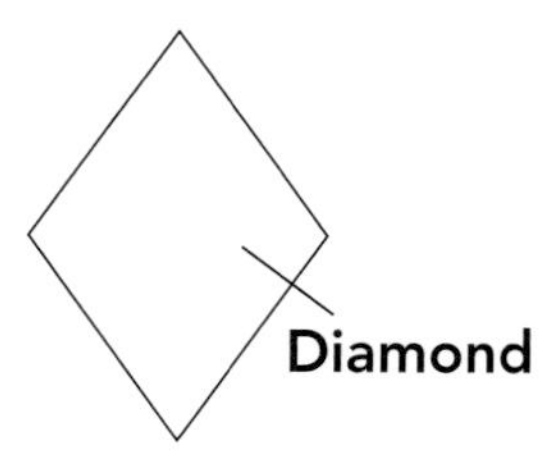

Dressy Napkin Holder

Fuse fabric onto a French-fry box for a fancy napkin holder.

Materials
- Cardboard French-fry container
- Aleene's Fusible Web™
- Print fabric
- Aleene's Tacky Glue™
- Clothespins
- Assorted trims: braid, ribbon, charm

Directions
1. **For napkin holder,** carefully open glued seams of container until it lies completely flat. Wipe both sides of container with damp paper towel to clean. Fuse web onto wrong side of 2 pieces of fabric, each large enough to cover 1 side of container. Place container right side down on web and trace shape onto each piece of fabric. Cut out each shape.

2. With edges aligned, fuse 1 fabric piece onto each side of container. Refold container into its original shape and glue flaps in place. Use clothespins to hold flaps in place until glue is dry. Referring to photo, glue assorted trims to front of napkin holder as desired.

3. **For napkin,** cut 1 (15") square of fabric. Fuse ½"-wide strips of web to each edge on wrong side of fabric square. Turn under ½" along each edge and fuse for hem.

Buffet Table Caddies

For your next buffet dinner, transform cardboard drink containers into attractive holders for silverware and napkins.

Materials

- **For each:** Cardboard drink-bottle container
- Flat black spray paint
- Aleene's Premium-Coat™ Acrylic Paints: Deep Fuchsia, Medium Fuchsia, True Yellow, Deep Violet, Gold, Blush, Black
- 1" square sponge
- Pop-up craft sponges
- Waxed paper
- Toothpick

Directions

1. Spray-paint cardboard container black. Let dry. **For hearts-and-stars holder,** sponge-paint container with Deep Fuchsia, using dampened 1" square sponge. Let dry. Rinse sponge thoroughly before dipping into different paint color. Transfer patterns to pop-up craft sponges and cut 1 heart and 1 star. **For angels holder,** sponge-paint container with Deep Violet, using dampened 1" square sponge. Let dry. Transfer patterns to pop-up craft sponges and cut 1 star, 1 dress, 1 wing, and 1 head.

2. Dip each sponge shape into water to expand and wring out excess water. Pour separate puddles of paint onto waxed paper. Dip 1 sponge into desired color of paint and blot excess paint on paper towel. Press sponge onto container to paint designs as desired. Let dry. **For hearts-and-stars holder,** paint hearts with Medium Fuchsia and stars with True Yellow. **For angels holder,** paint stars with True Yellow, dress with Medium Fuchsia, wings with Gold, and head with Blush. Use edge at 1 point of star sponge to paint True Yellow hair on angel's head. Use edge of wing sponge to paint Gold halo. Dip toothpick into Black and dot on head for eyes. Let dry.

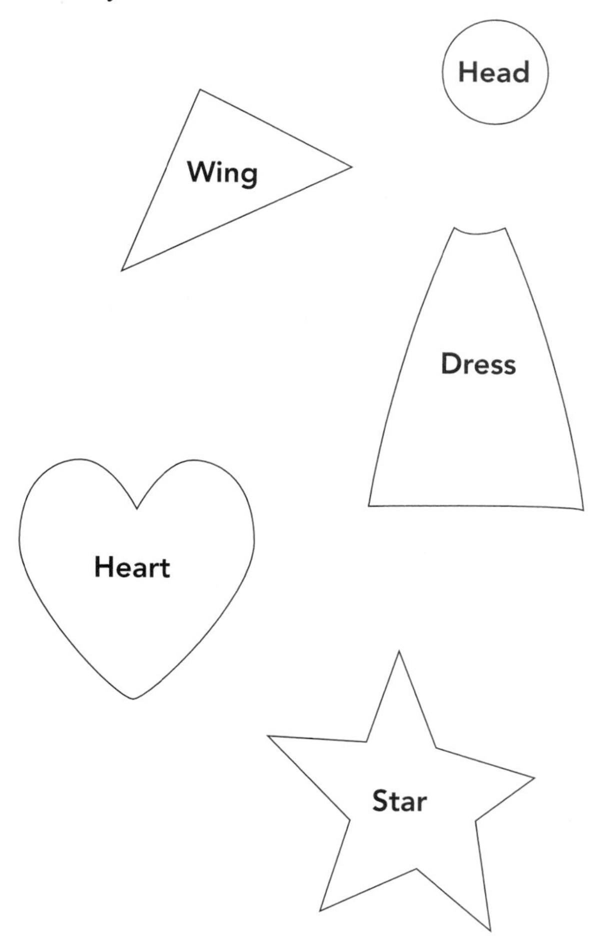

If you'd rather have a floral design on your buffet holder, use the patterns on pages 13 and 30 to cut flower shapes from the pop-up craft sponges. Make a caddy to match the Teatime Tray on page 40, using the patterns and the paint colors listed there.

Clay Tile Trivet

Sponge-paint topiary tree designs on a clay tile to make this trivet.

Materials

- 8"-square beige glazed clay tile
- Pop-up craft sponges
- Aleene's Premium-Coat™ Acrylic Paints: Deep Peach, Dusty Sage, Deep Beige, Deep Sage, Dusty Fuchsia, Soft Fuchsia
- Waxed paper
- Aleene's Premium Designer Brushes™: liner, shader
- Clear spray sealer
- 4 (3/4"-square) self-adhesive rubber bumper pads

Directions

1. Wash and dry glazed side of tile. Transfer patterns to pop-up craft sponges and cut 1 pot and 1 leaf. Dip each sponge shape into water to expand and wring out excess water.

2. Pour separate puddles of paint onto waxed paper. Dip pot sponge into Deep Peach and blot excess paint on paper towel. Referring to photo for positioning, press sponge onto tile to paint 1 pot on each edge of tile. Let dry.

3. Paint 1 Dusty Sage vine on each side of each pot, using liner brush. Paint 1 (5/8"-long) Deep Beige trunk above each pot, using liner brush. Let dry. Paint 1 (3/4"-diameter) Deep Sage circle at top of each trunk, using shader brush. Let dry. Dip dampened leaf sponge into Deep Sage and press onto tile to paint leaves along each side of each vine and on each painted circle (see photo). Let dry. Paint 1 Dusty Fuchsia bow on each tree, using liner brush. Paint several Dusty Fuchsia swirls on each tree as desired, using shader brush. While paint is still wet, dip clean brush into Soft Fuchsia and swirl on each Dusty Fuchsia area. Let dry.

4. Spray painted side of tile with 1 or 2 coats of sealer, letting dry between coats. Adhere 1 rubber bumper on wrong side of tile at each corner.

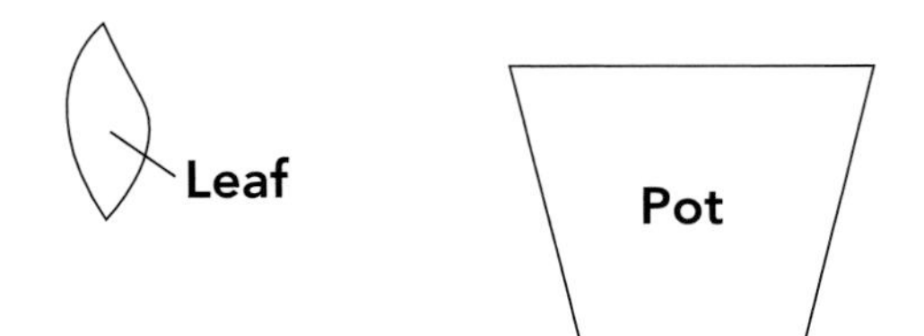

Select paint colors to match your kitchen or dining room to sponge-paint the designs on your trivet. For Christmas, paint bright green topiaries with colorful dots to represent ornaments.

CD-Cover Frames

Showcase your family photos with a gallery of these simple frames.

Materials

- **For each:** Photo
- Clear front cover from compact disc case
- Aleene's Tacky Glue™
- 18"-gauge florist's wire
- Raffia in desired color
- **For gift wrap frame:** Gift wrap
- **For heart frame:** 3" wooden heart
- Aleene's Enhancers™ All-Purpose Primer
- Aleene's Premium Designer Brush™: shader
- Aleene's Premium-Coat™ Acrylic Paint: Light Fuchsia
- Fabric scraps
- Ribbon in desired color

Directions for gift wrap frame

1. Tape photo in place on back of compact disc cover. Cut desired motifs from gift wrap. Arrange and glue motifs to front of compact disc cover as desired. Let dry.

2. Cut 1 (18") length of florist's wire. Wrap center of wire around pencil to coil, leaving 1½" free at each end. Remove pencil. Insert ¾" at 1 end of wire through each hole in top edge of compact disc cover, working from top to bottom. Bend up ends ¾". Tie raffia in bow around coiled hanger.

Directions for heart frame

1. Apply 1 coat of primer to wooden heart. Let dry. Paint heart with 1 or 2 coats of Light Fuchsia, letting dry between coats. Cut 1 (10") length of florist's wire. Bend wire at center, forming pointed hanger to fit compact disc cover. Insert ½" at 1 end of wire through each hole in top edge of compact disc cover, working from top to bottom. Bend wire ends as needed to secure hanger.

2. To attach heart to wire hanger, glue fabric pieces to back of heart, sandwiching wire in between. Let dry. Handling raffia and ribbon as 1, tie raffia and ribbon in bow. Glue bow to top front of heart. Let dry.

Elegant Dresser Set

Lace, beads, charms, ribbons, and other trims convert outdated dresser accessories into an opulent display.

Materials

- **For each:** Aleene's Designer Tacky Glue™
- Assorted trims: ribbon roses, gold charms, pearls, beads, buttons
- **For mirror:** Hand mirror
- White paper
- 1 (8¼" x 12") piece ivory moiré fabric
- 1 (6¼"-diameter) circle batting
- 26" length ½"-wide ivory flat braid
- ⅛"-wide ivory satin ribbon: 1 (8") length, 1 (36") length
- 28" length 1¼"-wide ivory trim with leaf motif
- 4"-diameter gold metallic doily
- Florist's wire scrap
- **For jewelry box:** Jewelry box
- Gold spray paint
- Ivory flat lace: 1 (8½" x 12") piece, 1 (5" x 35") strip
- 2 (36") lengths ½"-wide ivory flat braid
- 36" length 1"-wide ivory trim with bow motif
- 6"-diameter gold metallic doily
- 22" length 1⅛"-wide ivory wired-edged ribbon
- **For cotton-ball holder:** Cotton-ball holder or small box with lid
- Ivory moiré fabric: 1 (4¼"-diameter) circle, 1 (4" x 11½") strip
- 11¼" length ½"-wide ivory decorative trim
- Ivory flat braid: 1 (9") length, 1 (11") length
- 1 (1¾" x 11") strip batting
- 11¼" length 1¼"-wide ivory trim with leaf motif

Directions for mirror

Note: Mirror shown is 6¼" wide at top and 10½" long. Adjust fabric and trim requirements as needed to fit your mirror.

1. If needed, clean mirror frame. To make patterns, trace entire mirror frame and then trace handle portion only onto white paper. Cut out patterns. Transfer patterns to fabric and cut out, adding 1" all around frame piece. Glue batting circle to back of mirror frame. Center frame, batting side down, on mirror frame fabric. Fold and glue excess fabric to front of frame, clipping curves and trimming excess fabric around mirror as needed. Glue handle fabric to front of frame handle, covering raw fabric edges. Let dry.

2. With edge of braid aligned with edge of frame, glue flat braid to front of mirror frame, covering raw fabric edges. Let dry. Tie 8" ribbon length in bow. Glue bow to front of mirror frame at top of handle. Let dry.

3. With bound edge of trim aligned with edge of mirror frame, glue leaf trim to back of mirror. Center and glue doily on back of mirror. Make multilooped bow with 36" ribbon length, securing bow with florist's wire. Glue bow on top of doily. Glue assorted trims to back of mirror as desired. Let dry.

Fabric and lace trims in shades of ivory cover this hand mirror with a combination of textures. A gold metallic doily, treasured charms, and loose pearls add elegance to this timeless design.

Directions for jewelry box

Note: Box shown is 7" wide, 10" long, and 3½" deep, including hinged lid. Adjust flat lace and trim requirements as needed to fit your jewelry box.

1. If needed, clean box. Spray-paint entire outside surface of box gold. Let dry. Center lid of box on 8½" x 12" piece of lace. Fold and glue lace to inside of lid, mitering corners and trimming lace around hinges and clasp as needed. Let dry. With 1 long edge of lace even with top edge of box, wrap and glue lace strip around box sides, trimming lace around hinges and clasp as needed. Fold and glue excess lace to bottom of box, mitering corners. Let dry.

2. With edge of braid aligned with bottom edge of lid, wrap and glue 1 braid length around sides of lid, trimming braid around hinges and clasp as needed. With edge of braid aligned with top edge of box, wrap and glue 1 braid length around sides of box, trimming braid around hinges and clasp as needed. Let dry. With bound edge of trim aligned with edge of lid, glue bow trim around top of lid. Center and glue doily on lid. Tie ribbon in bow. Glue bow on top of doily. Glue assorted trims to box lid as desired. Let dry.

Directions for cotton-ball holder

Note: Holder shown is 3¾" diameter and 2" high. If you prefer to make cotton-ball holder, use small round cardboard box with plastic or cardboard lid. Center and cut 1 (⅞"-diameter) hole in lid. Cover box and lid as described below, adjusting fabric and trim requirements as needed to fit your box and lid.

1. Center lid right side down on 4¼" circle of fabric. Fold and glue excess fabric to wrong side of lid, clipping curves as needed. Let dry. Clip center of fabric at hole in lid. Fold and glue excess fabric around edge of hole to wrong side of lid. Let dry. Glue bound edge of decorative trim around lid so that trim extends below lid. With edge of braid aligned with edge of lid, glue 9" braid length around top of lid. Let dry. If desired, glue assorted trims to lid. Let dry.

2. Wrap and glue batting around sides of box. With 1" of fabric extending above top edge of box, wrap and glue fabric strip around box. Fold and glue excess fabric to inside and bottom of box, clipping curves as needed. Let dry. With bound edge of trim aligned with bottom edge of box, glue leaf trim around sides of box. Glue remaining braid length around sides of box at bottom, covering bound edge of trim. Let dry.

Natural Touches

Tiny topiaries, featuring moss, berries, dried flowers, and foliage, flank a candlestick lamp. For the lampshade, cover an existing shade with a brown grocery bag and then glue on moss, natural items, and butterflies cut from gift wrap.

Materials

- **For each:** Aleene's Designer Tacky Glue™
- Sheet moss
- **For rose topiary:** Small plastic cap (about 2½" in diameter and 2" high)
- Aleene's Premium-Coat™ Acrylic Paints: Deep Peach, Gold
- Sponge paintbrush
- 7½" length wooden skewer
- Styrofoam: block to fit inside cap, 1 (1½"-diameter) ball
- Aleene's Preserved Flowers and Foliage™: ming fern, gypsophilia
- Tiny rosebuds
- White sheer fabric scraps
- Metallic threads: red, pink
- Pearl-headed corsage pins
- **For berries topiary:** Small plastic cup (about 1½" in diameter at top and 1⅝" high)
- Gold spray paint
- 5½" length wooden skewer
- Styrofoam block to fit inside cup
- Cork from wine bottle
- Aleene's Preserved Flowers and Foliage™: boxwood
- Assorted natural materials: tiny pinecones, berries, small seedpods
- **For lampshade:** Lampshade
- Brown grocery bag
- Butterfly gift wrap
- 3" square cardboard squeegee
- Assorted natural materials: tiny pinecones, berries, small seedpods, cloves, star anise, acorns

Directions for rose topiary

1. Wash and dry plastic cap. Paint plastic cap with 1 or 2 coats of Deep Peach, letting dry between coats. Paint wooden skewer Gold. Let dry. Glue foam block inside cap. Dip 1 end of skewer into glue and push into foam block. Dip free end of skewer into glue and push halfway into foam ball. Let dry.

2. Glue moss to cover ball and foam in cap. Glue fern pieces, gypsophilia sprigs, and rosebuds to moss-covered ball and base of topiary as desired (see photo).

3. Cut sheer fabric into several ½" x 1" strips. Cut several 5" lengths from red metallic thread. Tie each 5" thread length in bow. Fold and gather center of 1 fabric strip. Pin gathered area of fabric strip and 1 red metallic bow to moss-covered ball, using 1 corsage pin (see photo). Repeat to pin additional fabric strips and red metallic bows to topiary as deisred. Cut 1 (20") length of each color of metallic thread. Handling both thread lengths as 1, fold threads to create several loops of various lengths. Pin thread loops to bottom of moss-covered ball.

Directions for berries topiary

1. Wash and dry plastic cup. Spray-paint cup and wooden skewer gold. Let dry. Glue foam block inside cup. Dip 1 end of skewer into glue and push into foam block. Dip free end of skewer into glue and push halfway into cork. Let dry.

2. Glue moss to cover foam ball and foam in cup. Glue boxwood pieces and assorted natural materials to topiary as desired. Let dry.

Directions for lampshade

1. Starting at seam, roll shade on flattened grocery bag and mark bottom edge of shade as you roll. Realign shade and repeat to mark top edge. Draw line connecting top and bottom lines at each end of pattern. Cut out, adding ½" all around. To cover shade, center shade on brown bag piece. Starting at seam, apply glue to shade and gently roll shade on brown bag. Continue around shade, smoothing brown bag as you go. Overlap and glue ends of brown bag. Let dry. Fold top and bottom edges of brown bag to inside of shade and glue, clipping curves as needed. Let dry.

2. Glue gift wrap to 1 layer of remaining grocery bag, using squeegee to apply thin coat of glue between layers. Let dry for about 5 minutes. Cut desired number of butterfly motifs from layered paper. While glue is still wet, shape butterflies to add dimension. Let dry. Glue sprigs of moss around top and bottom edges of shade. Glue butterfly cutouts and assorted natural materials to shade as desired. Let dry.

Tiny topiaries are at home in many settings. Display them on a dressing table, a mantel, or a bedside table to add a natural touch to your decor. Make a forest of topiaries and arrange them as a centerpiece for a dinner party.

Decorative Birdhouses

Look in your yard for many of the items needed to create these designs.

Materials

- **For each:** Pint-sized cardboard milk carton or quart-sized square plastic jug
- Aleene's Designer Tacky Glue™
- Craft knife
- Desired color Aleene's Premium-Coat™ Acrylic Paint
- Sponge paintbrush
- Assorted natural materials: pinecone scales, tiny pinecones, star anise, acorns, twigs, berries
- Sheet moss

Directions for 1 birdhouse

1. Wash and dry carton or jug. Glue carton opening closed or glue lid onto jug. Let dry. Cut 1 ($1\frac{1}{8}$"-diameter) circle in 1 side of carton or jug for birdhouse door, using craft knife. Paint carton or jug with 1 or 2 coats of paint, letting dry between coats.

2. **To complete carton birdhouse,** glue pinecone scales to top of carton for roof shingles. Glue small pieces of pinecone scales around door of birdhouse. Glue small sprigs of moss and other assorted natural materials to birdhouse as desired. Let dry. **To complete jug birdhouse,** glue sheet moss to top of jug for roof. Glue additional moss and other assorted natural materials to birdhouse as desired. Let dry.

Decoupaged Frame & Box

Save unused tickets from a fair or a raffle and glue them onto a box or a frame.

Materials

- **For each:** Black spray paint
- Aleene's Tacky Glue™
- 3" square cardboard squeegee
- Assorted tickets in desired colors
- Clear spray sealer (optional)
- **For frame:** 2 (8" x 10") pieces lightweight cardboard
- **For box:** Papier-mâché box

Directions

1. Center and cut 1 ($4\frac{7}{8}$" x 7") rectangle from 1 piece of cardboard for frame. Set cutout aside for another use. Spray-paint frame, box, and lid black. Let dry.

2. Squeegee thin coat of glue on right side of frame. Working in diagonal rows, press strips of tickets into glue, trimming strip ends even with frame edges. Let dry. In same manner, glue strips of tickets to sides of box and to top and sides of lid. If desired, spray frame, box, and lid with 1 or 2 coats of sealer, letting dry between coats. Glue remaining piece of cardboard to back of frame, leaving 1 end open to insert picture. Let dry.

Sunny Window Ornaments

Brighten a window with one or more of these suncatchers. When the sun shines through the tissue paper designs, it brings them to life.

Materials

- **For each:** Clear plastic cover from computer software package (about 6⅜" wide and 6½" long)
- Aleene's Reverse Collage Glue™
- Aleene's Premium Designer Brush™: shader
- Aleene's 3-D Foiling Glue™
- Aleene's Gold Craft Foil™
- Aleene's Designer Tacky Glue™
- **For stars suncatcher:** 1 (5⅝" x 6") piece star print tissue paper
- Faceted plastic beads: 2 (4-mm) clear, 1 (6-mm) pink, 1 (8-mm) clear, 2 (8-mm) lavender
- Jewelry findings: 1 eye pin, 1 (3-mm) jump ring, 1 (8-mm) jump ring, 1 (5") length gold beading wire
- Needlenose pliers
- Gold heart charm
- Aleene's Satin Sheen Twisted Ribbon™: pink
- **For sun suncatcher:** Aleene's Tissue Paper™: light orange, medium yellow, light yellow
- Aleene's Satin Sheen Twisted Ribbon™: yellow

Directions for stars suncatcher

1. Remove paper or stickers from software cover. Open cover and lay flat on work surface with right side down. Brush coat of Reverse Collage Glue on inside front cover. Press print tissue paper facedown into glue-covered area. Brush coat of Reverse Collage Glue on top of tissue paper, pressing out any air bubbles. Let dry.

2. Close software cover. Referring to page 5, make tape tip for bottle of 3-D Foiling Glue. Outline tissue paper motifs and add details on right side of cover, using 3-D Foiling Glue. Let dry. (Glue will be opaque and sticky when dry. Glue must be thoroughly dry before foil is applied.)

3. To apply gold foil, lay foil dull side down on top of glue lines. Using finger, gently but firmly press foil onto glue, completely covering glue with foil. Peel away foil paper. If any part of glue is not covered, reapply foil as needed.

4. For beaded dangle at bottom of suncatcher, thread 1 (4-mm) clear bead, pink bead, and remaining 4-mm clear bead on eye pin. Form free end of eye pin into small loop. Attach heart charm to 1 loop of eye pin, using 3-mm jump ring and pliers. Center and poke 1 hole in bottom edge of suncatcher. Attach beaded dangle to hole, using 8-mm jump ring and pliers.

5. For hanger, insert 1 end of wire through hole at top of suncatcher. Bend up ¾" at same end of wire. Thread remaining beads onto wire, pushing first bead down over bent up end of wire. Bend down free end of wire, pushing end of wire inside top bead and leaving ¾" loop for hanger.

6. Cut 1 (16") length of twisted ribbon. Untwist ribbon. Tear ribbon into narrow lengthwise strips. Handling several strips as 1, tie strips in bow. Glue bow to front of suncatcher at top, using Designer Tacky Glue. Let dry.

Directions for sun suncatcher

1. Transfer pattern on page 138 to tissue paper and cut 1 sun each from light orange and medium yellow. Cut 1 (5⅝" x 6") piece of light yellow tissue paper for background. Remove paper or stickers from software cover. Open cover and lay flat on work surface with right side down.

2. Brush coat of Reverse Collage Glue on inside front cover. Center and press light orange sun onto glue-covered area. Brush coat of Reverse Collage Glue on top of light orange sun, pressing out any air bubbles. Referring to photo for positioning, press medium yellow sun into wet glue on top of light orange sun. Brush coat of Reverse Collage Glue on top of medium yellow sun. Repeat to glue light yellow background piece in place on top of sun design, brushing top of background paper with coat of glue. Let dry.

3. Referring to Step 3 of stars suncatcher, outline sun and draw face on right side of cover with 3-D Foiling Glue. Referring to Step 4 of stars suncatcher, apply foil to glue.

4. Refer to Step 6 of stars suncatcher to make bow with yellow twisted ribbon. For hanger, thread 1 remaining narrow strip of twisted ribbon through hole at top of suncatcher and knot ends. Glue bow to front of suncatcher at top, using Designer Tacky Glue. Let dry.

Kitchen Canisters

Old metal canisters get a new look with pastel hearts and floral teacups cut from paper napkins.

Materials

- **For each:** Metal canister with lid
- Flat white spray paint
- Aleene's Premium-Coat™ Acrylic Paints: Ivory, Soft Sage, Medium Yellow, Medium Fuchsia, True Fuchsia, Light Fuchsia, Medium Violet, Soft Green
- Aleene's Premium Designer Brushes™: shader, liner
- Print paper napkins: floral heart, teacup
- Aleene's Paper Napkin Appliqué Glue™
- Clear spray polyurethane finish

Directions

1. **For each canister,** wash and dry canister and lid. Spray-paint canister and lid white to prime. Let dry. Paint canister and handle on lid with 1 or 2 coats of Ivory for base coat, letting dry between coats. Paint lid with 1 or 2 coats of Soft Sage for base coat, letting dry between coats.

2. Cut desired motifs from paper napkins. Remove bottom plies of napkins to leave cutouts 1-ply thick. Working over small area at a time, brush coat of glue on canister in desired position. Press 1 cutout into glue-covered area, pressing out any air bubbles. Brush coat of glue on top of cutout. Repeat to apply additional cutouts to canister as desired. Let dry.

3. Referring to photo, paint flowers and leaves on canister and lid handle, using liner brush and desired paint colors. Dip handle of liner brush into Medium Yellow and press on canister or lid handle to paint center of each flower. Let dry. Dip handle of shader brush into Medium Fuchsia and press on edge of lid to paint dots around lid. Let dry. Spray canister and lid with 1 or 2 coats of finish, letting dry between coats.

Paper napkin appliqué is an easy way to decorate all sorts of home decor items. Use this technique on baskets, cardboard or wooden boxes, or fabric items such as place mats or tea towels.

Colander Wind Chimes

All this design needs is a gentle breeze to stire the flattened spoons and the old keys dangling from the sponge-painted colander.

Materials
- Colander
- Flat black spray paint
- Waxed paper
- Aleene's Premium-Coat™ Acrylic Paints: Copper, Dusty Spruce, True Green, White
- Small sponge piece
- Clear spray sealer
- Metal washers: 2 (1"-diameter), 1 (2"-diameter)
- Aleene's Designer Tacky Glue™
- Fishing line
- 1 (2¾"-long) fishing weight
- Beads: 4-mm iridescent, 6-mm clear, assorted large decorative (See photo.)
- 2 (½") jump rings
- 1 (¾"-square) faux crystal
- Needlenose pliers
- 1 (2"-diameter) faux ivory charm
- 4 stainless iced teaspoons
- Hammer
- Drill with ⅛"-diameter bit
- 6 keys

Directions

1. Wash and dry colander. Spray-paint entire colander black for base coat. Place colander upside down on work surface covered with waxed paper. Sponge-paint colander with dampened sponge, using paint colors as desired. Spray colander with 1 or 2 coats of sealer, letting dry between coats.

2. To make clapper, center and glue 1 (1") washer on each side of 2" washer. Let dry. Cut 1 (48") length of fishing line. Knot 1 end of line to loop at 1 end of fishing weight. Thread 4-mm, 6-mm, and decorative beads onto line as desired, knotting line after last bead. Knot line 2¼" above previous knot. Thread 1 (4-mm) bead, 1 (6-mm) bead, and 1 decorative bead onto line. Thread washers onto line. Glue washers to decorative bead. Let dry. Thread 1 decorative bead onto line above washers. Glue washers to bead. Let dry. Thread 1 (6-mm) bead and 1 (4-mm) bead onto line, knotting line after last bead. Attach 1 jump ring to each hole in crystal, using pliers. Attach charm to 1 jump ring. Attach remaining jump ring to free loop of fishing weight.

3. For hanger, cut 1 (20") length of fishing line. Fold line in half. Working from outside of colander, thread folded end of line through hole at center bottom of colander. Thread 1 bead onto folded end of line. Thread free end of clapper line through folded end of line beneath bead and knot end around clapper line. Working from outside of colander, pull free ends of hanger line taut so that bead touches colander on inside. Handling both ends of line as 1, thread beads onto line as desired, knotting line ends after last bead. Knot line ends leaving 5" loop for hanging.

4. Working on hard protected work surface, hammer bowl of each spoon flat. Center and drill 1 hole through handle of each spoon. To make chime dangles, cut 10 (18") lengths of fishing line. For each dangle, knot spoon or key to 1 end of 1 length of fishing line. Thread beads onto line as desired, knotting line after last bead. Working from inside of colander, thread free end of line through 1 hole in colander, making sure spoon or key hangs even with washers of clapper. Thread 1 (6-mm) bead and 1 (4-mm) bead onto free end of line, knotting line after last bead. Trim excess line.

Flower Garden Wastebasket

A garden of bright blooms and busy bees decorates this wastebasket.